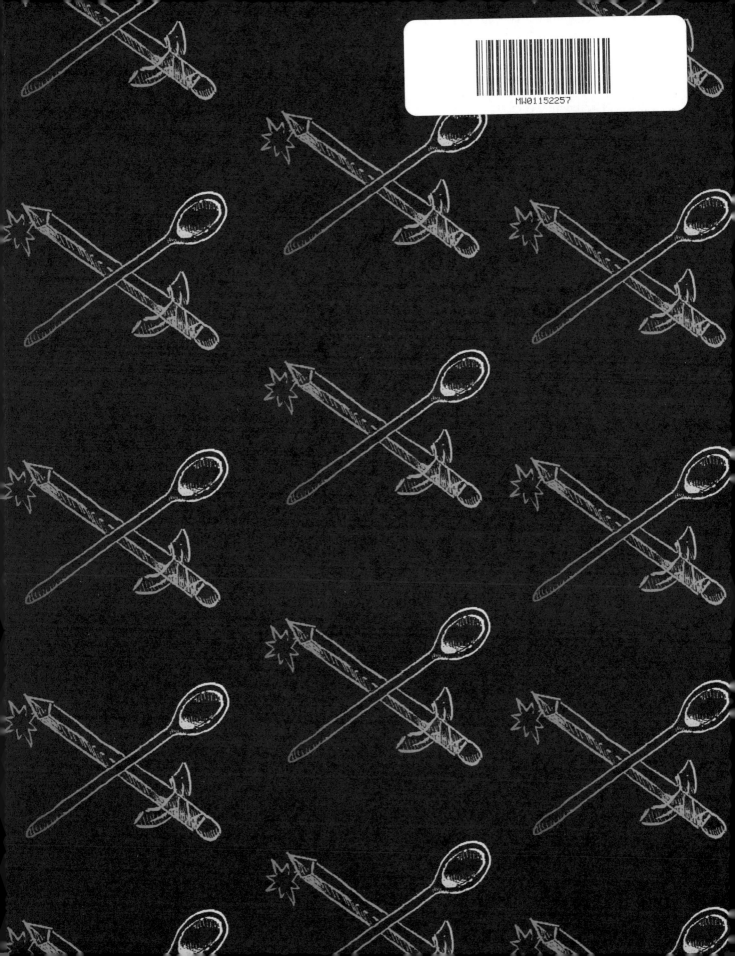

THE LEGEND'S COOKBOOK

Inspired Recipes by
Peter J. Abreu

The Legend's Cookbook

by Peter J. Abreu
(with a Little Help from His Friends)

THE LEGEND'S COOKBOOK

by Peter J. Abreu
(with a Little Help from His Friends)
Published by JOBJOB LLC
1st Edition

The Legend's Cookbook

"Making cooking an adventure."

The Legend's Cookbook is authored by Peter J. Abreu and written, edited, designed, and published by JobJob, LLC. This first edition was distributed by The Yetee, LLC in Aurora, IL.

Printed in PRC.
iSBN:
Ebook: 978-1-7345792-0-8 Hardback: 978-1-7345792-2-2 Paperback: 978-1-7345792-1-5

This cookbook is dedicated to my parents who always encouraged me to follow my dreams.

Table of Contents

Introduction

My name is Peter J. Abreu. I'm a chef, pilot, and traveler. Originally hailing from Long Island, NY, I can't say I'm from just there. My mother's Italian, my father's Cuban, and I learned almost everything I know about good food from watching my family cook dinners together. Everything else I learned about food came from my travels abroad. My parents worked in the airline industry as I was growing up, so I was fortunate enough to be able to embrace my heritage and experience others all across the globe. I spent my summers in high school teaching and cooking in the Castilian region of Spain, and that's where I realized my dream is to help spread what I'd learned all across the globe. I attended flight school, became a pilot, and started my own YouTube cooking show, *Cucco's Kitchen*, where I embrace my love for cooking, video games, and traveling. I've met a lot of incredible people on my travels, shared so many memorable meals, and learned a lot about what to do in the kitchen. What I love about a good meal is that it brings people together and takes them on a journey. I want to bring that to as many people as possible, and this cookbook will be your invitation to this journey.

Cooking isn't something that should be consigned to just the kitchen. Food is a part of all our lives and often times it is hurried, rushed, and half-baked. The Legend's Cookbook is a culinary adventure between two covers. We've filled this cookbook with good food, charming illustrations, and imaginative recipes. This cookbook is for everyone, beginners and pros. Drawing from a litany of inspirations, we capture a sense of adventure, novelty, and the wild. These dishes will transport the reader to new worlds, teaching them to cook with a plethora of different techniques, approaches, and flavors. From classical culinary styles of French, Spanish, and German, to modern-day techniques, this cookbook will be your guide to fantastic dining every day. It will act as a gateway to a diverse dining table and truly take your breath away.

We wanted to capture the feeling of a travel journal and field guide with this cookbook. We won't just share recipes, we'll share things that we've learned as well. Have you ever wondered why saffron is so expensive? What's a genoise cake? Why do we put salt on everything? Get equipped with all sorts of cooking hints as well as delightful anatomical sketches and little watercolor pieces tucked away in the corners of pages. This cookbook is fun, adventurous, and stands out–not just in the kitchen, but on your bookshelf. It's something special. Whether this is your first duel with cooking or you're a seasoned adventurer, we'll run the gambit from easy recipes that require you to only boil water to complex ones, such as folding and baking delicious, buttery croissants. We want it to be an inspiration for you to experiment in the kitchen, to use unfamiliar herbs and spices, and to change your life–one meal at a time. Don't worry, we have your back. If you have any questions, you can always reach me via Twitter at @pwnapplez.

-Peter J. Abreu

P.S. I also have to take a moment to tell you all that I couldn't have done this alone. I'm backed by an incredible team of artists, editors, photographers, and a sous chef that's saved my hide more times than I can count. I want to introduce you to Alyssa Browning, sous chef extraordinaire.

Hi! My name is Alyssa Browning, and I am the sous-chef for this cookbook. I have a job as a teaching assistant and I'm currently in culinary school to get my baking and pastry certificate. I enjoy all kinds of cooking. There's something about a beautifully crafted pastry that reaches to me not only as someone who loves food, but as an artist. You'll see some of my art throughout this book as well, which I hope you enjoy along with our many culinary creations. And, like Peter, if you need a helpful cooking tip, you can reach me via Twitter at @kiddytank.

-Alyssa Browning

Also hi! I'm Effie! But most people call me F3, the *Friendly Facts Fairy*. Basically, I went on this long crazy adventure with this adventurer guy and I learned a lot! I was kind of cooped up for most of it, like in a bottle, but I got out and now I can help you all out! Well, I was kind of let go... Some people say I'm obnoxious but I don't like those people. I'll be accompanying you now through this book and supplying you with all sorts of fun facts!

-Effie

-Li Kovács @LiKovacs 13

Kitchen Staples

Before you start cooking, you should have the ingredients you're planning to use on hand. Granted, on more than one occasion I've had to make the mad mid-baking dash to the grocery store to buy more butter, so let's just hope you're better at this whole "planning" thing than me. I want to outline a few kitchen staples, the essentials that you should probably always have in your pantry. Keep in mind that we don't use all of these ingredients in this book's recipes; but if you wanna make spaghetti, a batch of cookies, or a simple late night snack, these are what you should equip your kitchen with. Also, keep in mind that this is a general list. Availability, diet restrictions, and food preferences will always influence what's in your kitchen. Knowing what you like to eat and keeping it stocked in the pantry is what all true cooks strive for!

Dry Goods
— These are dried or preserved food items which have an extremely long shelf-life. Dry goods are often the cheapest and most used ingredients in your kitchen. If you buy them in bulk and keep them from getting wet, they'll save you from an empty stomach. Most of these are carbohydrates and where most of your daily caloric intake comes from.

• Flour	• Sugar	• Rice	• Cereal
• Cornstarch	• Dry Beans	• Pasta	• Coffee

Baking
— Ovens first appeared on the kitchen scene around 6,500 years ago. That means people have been baking for a long time. Over the millenia, people have perfected the craft with a handful of ingredients that no baker today would be caught dead without.

• Baking Soda	• Baking Powder	• Cocoa Powder	• Baking Chocolate
• Vanilla Extract	• Active Dry Yeast	• Vegetable Oil	• Olive Oil

Herbs, Spices, and Sauces
— Wars used to be fought over these things and today we often take for granted that they sit in little shakers on the corner of every kitchen table. Do not underestimate the power of a pinch of salt! Also, a lot of the flavor in spices can be improved or changed by grinding them fresh.

• Salt	• Black Pepper	• Chili Powder	• Red Pepper
• Curry Powder	• Hot Sauce	• Soy Sauce	• Basil
• Garlic	• Ground Cinnamon	• Ground Cumin	• Ground Ginger
• Oregano	• Paprika	• Mayonaise	• Mustard
• Rosemary	• Thyme	• Onion Powder	• Garlic Powder

Refrigerator Companions
— These items should populate the shelves of every fridge. When it comes to food, refrigerated items are the new kids on the block. With home refrigeration only coming onto the scene less than a century ago and still widely unavailable over large swaths of the globe, take a moment to treasure that jar of mayonnaise. Also, when it comes to things you store in the fridge, use your senses and common sense. If it looks weird, toss it out. If it smells bad, throw it away. If you hear it moving around, run away. Take your time to store your food properly in your fridge. Label your foods with dates. Good food is always better when you're certain it's safe.

• Milk	• Eggs	• Butter	• Cheese
• Fresh Vegetables	• Fresh Fruits	• Beef	• Chicken

Basic Equipment

Have you ever heard of the old saying, 'there's a tool for every job'? Well, lucky for you, there's actually like five tools for every job. However, I realized when trying to open a can with a spoon that maybe I should invest in some more kitchen equipment, so I gave up and bought a can opener. Needless to say, there are an infinite number of kitchen tools you can buy, but I like to keep a neat and tidy amount of them at my disposal. Too much stuff can lead to clutter, but my kitchen isn't yours. Stock up as you see fit, but I'm investing in that can opener.

Food Prep:
- Knife Set
- Cutting Board
- Mixing Bowls
- Colander
- Whisk
- Grater
- Shears
- Blender
- Glass Storage Containers
- Aluminum Foil
- Parchment Paper
- Sandwich Bags
- Electric Mixer
- Food Processor
- Immersion Blender

Utensils:
- Ladle
- Spatula
- Slotted Spoon
- Wooden Spoon
- Tongs
- Can Opener
- Timer
- Candy Thermometer
- Cooking Towel
- Potholder
- Trivet
- Dry Ingredients Measuring Cups
- Wet Ingredients Measuring Cups
- Measuring Spoons

Cookware:
- Skillet
- Small Saucepan
- Sauté Pan with Lid
- Large Pot
- Stockpot
- Baking Sheet Pan
- Baking Rack
- Cake Pan
- Pie Tin
- Glass Baking Dish
- Dutch Oven

Chef's Knife:

This is your best friend in the kitchen. Use it to cut meat, chop vegetables, and do everything in between. Equip this as your main item.

Cleaver:

The most iconic knife of the butcher. This tool has little use in the modern kitchen. Unless you're hewing chunks of flesh off the bone, this knife will often just be consigned to sitting in your butchers block until it rusts.

Paring Knife:

This smaller, simpler, sharper blade is for the delicate world of peeling fruit and vegetables.

Santoku Knife:

The Eastern version of the Western-style chef's knife. Santoku means "three virtues": slicing, dicing, and mincing. The hollows on the side of the knife help prevent ingredients from sticking. It can do pretty much anything a chef's knife can do.

Bread Knife:

Bread knife cuts bread. It is also a knife. Bread Knife.

Sandwich Knife:

A gradual evolution of the bread knife. Use it for slicing softer things. It works great for tomatoes, bread, cheese, and spreading mayo, it's the perfect sandwich-making tool! It also has a lot of utility, so make sure you have one on hand.

Steak Knife:

A steak knife will usually populate the dining room and not so much the kitchen. It is useful for cutting most ingredients and foods as well as spreading things like butter.

Butter Knife:

Use this for when you don't trust yourself to spread butter with a steak knife.

Boning Knife:

Thin and sharp, this curved blade is designed to get into small spaces to detach meat from bone. However, it has a new lease on life in the vegetarian's kitchen because it is also fantastic for peeling and cutting thin veggies.

Measurements

Mistakes are just learning opportunities, but if I had a rupee for every cake I accidentally ruined by mixing up tablespoons with teaspoons, well, let's just say I'd be a rich man. I always have to double-check my measurements and make sure everything is correct. When in doubt, use our helpful conversion chart in the back of the book, but here are some quick references to help you out and hopefully you'll keep them in mind.

1 tablespoon = 3 teaspoons = 15 milliliters
4 tablespoons = ¼ cup = 60 milliliters
1 fluid ounce = 2 tablespoons = 30 milliliters
1 cup = 8 fluid ounces = 240 milliliters
1 pint = 2 cups = 480 milliliters
1 quart = 4 cups = 950 milliliters
1 quart = .95 liters (Basically Equal)
1 quart = 2 pints = 950 milliliters
1 gallon = 4 quarts = 3800 milliliters = 3.8 liters
Tablespoon = tbsp
Teaspoon = tsp
Ounce = oz
Inch = "
Pound(s) = lb(s)

1 tablespoon = 3 teaspoons (15 milliliters)

2 Tablespoons = 1 Fluid Ounce (30 milliliters)

Keeping track of the heat on the stove or the oven is difficult. We will often refer to putting something on a medium heat or low heat, figuring exactly where that is on your equipment will need a bit of troubleshooting. As a good rule of thumb, we try to use this chart. Older and dirtier stoves will usually run cooler. The environment and elevation you're cooking in will also affect cooking time and temperature. When in doubt use your eyes, nose, and a cooking thermometer to make sure that you cook your meals to your liking!

Fahrenheit	Celsius	Stove Mark	Term
275°F	140°C	1	Warm
300°F	150°C	2	Very Low
325°F	165°C	3	Low
350°F	177°C	4	Medium Low
375°F	190°C	5	Medium
400°F	200°C	6	Medium High
425°F	220°C	7	High
450°F	230°C	8	High
475°F	245°C	9	Very High
500°F	260°C	10	Highest

Common Terms

We're going to use a lot of funny terms in this cookbook. Cooking is a universal constant among all cultures, regions, and people. Because of that, there is a lot of mixing of different culinary styles, traditions, and languages. As a result, there might be a handful of unfamiliar words that you might not have ever been exposed to. This is a little primer but we urge you to continue your culinary education. There's always a new dish out there that is a few hours of research away from becoming your new favorite. Let's just help you out on the beginning of what I think will be a lifelong quest for the perfect meal.

Bake – Cooking by dry heat, usually in an oven.

Barbecue – Grilling over an open fire through long, slow, and direct heat cooking, usually with lots of barbecue sauce.

Baste – Moistening foods with fat or other liquids while cooking to prevent drying out and to add flavor.

Beat – Mixing foods thoroughly to a smooth, even consistency, usually with a tool or implement.

Blanch – Briefly boiling fruits or vegetables to lock in color and flavor and then stopping the cooking with a quick submersion in cold water.

Blend – Mixing two or more ingredients, not as thoroughly as beating.

Boil – Heating a liquid until bubbles rise continually to the surface.

Braise – Gently cooking food in a small amount of liquid in a covered pan.

Broil – Cooking while exposed to a direct heat source, usually on a rack or spit in an oven or stove.

Bruise – Crushing an ingredient to release the flavors or oils.

Caramelize – Cooking food or a sugar until it is brown and shiny.

Chop – Cutting ingredients into rough ½" to ¾" squares.

Core – To cut out or remove the fibrous core of something, usually fruits or vegetables.

Cream – Softening a fat, usually butter, by beating it at room temperature until it forms a rich, smooth cream.

Crumb – Coating food in breadcrumbs or other crumbs in preparation for frying or baking.

Devein – Removing the blue-black digestive tract from the back of some shellfish with a knife.

Dice – Finely cutting ingredients into rough ⅛" to ½" squares.

Drizzle – Sprinkling drops of a liquid or syrup lightly over a food.

Dust – To top or decorate food with a fine, powdered coating of something, usually through a sieve.

Fold – Lightly mixing ingredients together while trying to keep their individual consistencies.

Fry – Cooking food in hot fat.

Garnish – Decorating a dish either to make it more aesthetically appealing or to add more flavor.

Grease – Covering a cooking surface with butter or oil to prevent sticking.

Knead – Working dough in a rough way with your hands to merge the ingredients.

Julienne – Cutting food into long, thin strips.

Marinade – A flavored liquid often used to soak a protein to help season it before cooking.

Marinate – To soak something in a marinade.

Mince – Very finely cutting ingredients into rough squares smaller than ⅛".

Mix – Stirring ingredients together.

Parboil – Partially cooking food by gently boiling it.

Peel – Removing the skin of a fruit or vegetable.

Pinch – A small amount that would fit between your finger and thumb.

Poach – Cooking food by submerging it in seasoned simmering liquid.

Reduce – Boiling a food or liquid so that water evaporates and the end result thickens and concentrates.

Sauté – Cooking food in a small amount of fat over high heat in a shallow pan, turning often so the food cooks evenly.

Sear – Browning the surface of meat over a high temperature very quickly to seal in the flavor.

Season – Adding salt, pepper, and other spices or herbs.

Seasoning to Taste – Adding salt, pepper, and other spices or herbs until you think it tastes good.

Simmer – Heating a liquid just below its boiling point so that tiny bubbles form on the inside of the pot.

Slice – Cutting ingredients into uniformly shaped, large, flat pieces.

Steep – Submerging ingredients in warm or hot water, below the boiling point.

Stew – Slowly cooking ingredients by simmering in a small amount of liquid for a long time.

Stir-fry – Cooking food in a small amount of oil while constantly tossing or moving it in the pan or wok.

Whisk – Using an implement to incorporate as much air as possible into the mixture so it is light and airy.

Substitutions

Have you ever had to fight off an enemy horde with only a shovel and a handful of makeshift arrows? Well, cooking is like that sometimes. You might be out of eggs, or you might not want to use eggs! Dietary restrictions and pantry spaces effect everything you cook, so we want to try to help you out. Using different ingredients will affect the outcome of your dish—be it in texture, taste, or otherwise—but we urge you to experiment. Maybe add a banana to your cookies instead of egg—you might find something you like better than the normal recipe. Also, if you are worried, concerned, or just want more information about ingredient inclusion or exclusion, please talk to your doctor or nutritionist.

Baking Substitutions:

1 tsp Lemon Juice = ½ tsp Vinegar
1 tsp Lemon Zest = ½ tsp Lemon Extract
1 tsp Baking Powder = ¼ tsp Baking Soda + ½ tsp Cream of Tartar
1 cup Unsalted Butter = 1 cup Shortening
1 Egg = ½ Banana

Cooking Substitutions:

1 tsp Cornstarch = 2 tsp Flour
1 clove Garlic = ⅛ tsp Garlic Powder
½ cup Soy Sauce = 4 tbsp Worcestershire Sauce
Soy Sauce = Coconut Aminos
White Wine = Chicken Broth
Red Wine = Beef Broth
Meat = Mushrooms

Sugar Substitutes:

1 cup Honey = ¾ cup Sugar + ¼ cup Water
1 cup Brown Sugar = 1 cup Granulated Sugar + ¼ cup Molasses
1 cup Powdered Sugar = 1 cup Sugar + ⅓ tsp Cornstarch
1 tsp Sugar = 6 drops Liquid Stevia = 1¼ tsp Erythritol
1 cup Sugar = ⅔ cup Agave Nectar

Spice Substitutions:

Saffron = Ground Turmeric
Ground Cumin = Chili Powder
1 tsp Garam Masala = 1 tsp Ground cumin + ¼ tsp Ground Allspice
2 tsp Pumpkin Pie Spice = 1 tsp Ground Allspice + ¼ tsp Ground Nutmeg
½ tsp Ground Cinnamon = ¼ tsp Ground Nutmeg = ¼ tsp Ground Allspice
1 tsp Ground Allspice = ½ tsp Ground Cinnamon + ¼ tsp Ground Ginger + ¼ tsp Ground Cloves
1 tbsp Italian Seasoning = 1 tsp Ground Basil + 1 tsp Ground Oregano + 1 tsp Ground Rosemary
Ground Ginger = Ground Nutmeg
Basil = Oregano

Dietary Substitutions:

Butter = Avocado
Flour = Black Bean Flour
Bread Crumbs = Almond Flour
Beef = Portobello Mushrooms
Shellfish = Imitation Crab
Chicken = Tofu

Handling a Knife

In the kitchen, the knife is your main weapon. Not only do you need a good, sturdy knife, but you need to know how to handle it. If you don't, not only are you going to have a hard time on food prep, but you are also liable to hurt yourself or others. Knives—just like hot surfaces and boiling liquids—need to be respected in the kitchen. So a lot of these knife handling skills focus more on handling yourself before you even touch a knife.

Knife Safety:

• Keep knives sharp. Dull knives will make cooking a chore.
• Never touch the sharp blade of a knife. If you are unsure if a knife is sharp, just sharpen it again.
• Use a knife only for its intended purpose. Also, use the right knife for the right occasion if you have them. Don't use a bread knife on a roast!
• Make sure your cutting board is on a stable surface. It can help to put a damp cloth under it to prevent it from slipping.
• When not actively cutting, place the knife down on a flat and safe surface. Don't carry it around the kitchen.
• Never place knives near the edge of a counter, they can fall off.
• Never leave a knife soaking in a sink of water, especially if the water is dirty and you can't see it.
• Don't use a knife with a broken handle, blade guard, or knuckle guard.

• Let a falling knife fall. Step back. Your first instinct is to reach out and try to catch it. Don't.
• Carry knives with the cutting edge angled slightly away from your body, with the tip pointed down to your side.
• Do not hand off a knife. Place it down and instruct the other person to pick it up.
• Store knives properly and safely in racks, butcher blocks, or drawers.
• Cut away from your body, if you don't, you will cut yourself. It seems intuitive to cut by pulling the blade towards your body but don't. Practice will make this second nature.
• If you're worried about cutting yourself, get a nice pair of cut resistant gloves.
• When you're cutting, keep your eyes on what you're cutting. Try not to have conversations or watch cooking videos. Use wireless headphones or speaker (we suggest getting yourself a GENKI Bluetooth adapter) if you need music while you cook.

Handle Grip:

This is the most intuitive way to hold a knife but you'd be surprised to find that it isn't always the best way. Use your dominant hand to grab the handle of the knife, that's it. That's the handle grip. It is very good for cutting soft ingredients but make sure you use your non-dominant hand to secure the blade.

Blade Grip:

This is the professional way to hold a knife, that's why it is also known as the "chef's grip". This grip requires you to pinch and control the blade between your curled pointer finger and thumb while using your other fingers to grab the handle. The positioning of the thumb and index finger allows you to control the blade with a greater level of precision. Think of this like holding a pencil. You can then use your other hand to stabilize the blade or hold what you're cutting.

Mincing:

To mince ingredients, you'll need both hands. Place the tip of your knife on the cutting board and hold it in place with your non-dominant hand, planting it right above what you intend to mince. After you secure the point, move the handle up and down with your dominant hand and mince your ingredients to a fine pile.

Meat Cuts

Not all meat is made equal. And I'm not talking about how pork is better than chicken, even though it is—debate me. I'm talking about how a T-bone cooks, tastes, and even looks fundamentally different from a flank steak, despite the fact that they come from the same animal. There are far more cuts and types of meat than what we have here but this is what you will usually find when you go down to your local supermarket.

Beef - This is the meat from cattle or cows (*Bos taurus*). You can find this meat in nearly every supermarket across North America and it has been a staple in people's diets ever since their original domestication over 10,000 years ago. One thing you might want to notice is the grade of the beef you're buying. In the USA, the USDA governmental agency grades beef on quality. Beef is graded either Prime, Choice, Select, Standard, Commercial, Utility, Cutter, or Canner. You don't really want to go below Select. **Trust me.**

When cooking beef, be mindful of the internal temperatures. This determines "doneness".

← **Rare is 120°F, 50°C.** The center is bright red and pink towards the edges. The entire thing is soft to the touch.

← **Medium Rare is 130°F, 55°C.** The center is very pink and a little brown on the edges. It is still soft but the edges are firm.

← **Medium is 140°F, 60°C.** The center is light pink while the outer portion is brown. It is starting to firm up.

← **Medium Well is 150°F, 65°C.** It is mostly gray-brown throughout with a touch of pink at the core. The entire piece is firm to touch.

← **Well Done is 160°F, 70°C and up.** It is gray-brown throughout with no pink. It feels firm and yields very little. Please don't order a steak Well Done.

CHUCK 7-BONE

Chuck: This is your cheap value steak, but that doesn't mean it should be overlooked. It's used in a lot of dishes, ranging from pot roast to hamburger. Full of connective tissue, it will fall apart when cooked.

SHOULDER TOP
BLADE STEAK
(FLAT IRON)

RIB STEAK

Rib: Ribs are, well, the ribs of the cow. Small, tender cuts with lots of fat in-between. There's a lot of flavor here.

Flat-iron: This long, flat steak is tasty, tender, and easy to cook. Great for beginners because it is cheap (it is technically part of the chuck.) That means you can afford to make a mistake or two.

SHANK CROSS CUT

BRISKET FLAT CUT

BRISKET

Shank: Think of the shank as the bicep of the animal. It has very low fat content and is incredibly tough, just like me (this is Peter, by the way). The best way to eat it is to braise it.

Brisket: Brisket is the fatty, tough chest area of the cow. Even though that sounds kind of gross, if you pair those characteristics with a slow and low fire, you have an award-winning meal. Slap on some dry rub and throw it in the slow cooker.

FLANK

Flank: Coming from the area right below the loin, this cut lacks bones and is incredibly lean. This cut is rising in popularity and price, as modern consumers are seeking leaner meats due to fat-cutting trends in diets. However, fat is flavor. Keep that in mind.

Tongue: Beef tongue might be a weird one but this part of the cow is incredibly tender and fatty.

TONGUE

TENDERLOIN STEAK

EYE ROUND STEAK

BOTTOM ROUND ROAST

Filet Mignon: AKA, tenderloin. This is the most tender cut from a cow, coming from the center of the loin area. The muscle doesn't bear any animal's body weight, making it soft and delicate. On average, a full-grown cow will only have about one pound's worth of filet mignon in it. Despite how desirable and expensive this cut is, it actually lacks flavor. This is why restaurants sell it wrapped in bacon to cover that up! And to charge you more!

Round: Lean and cheap, round comes from the cow's hind legs. Often times it gets turned into ground round, a fun phrase to say but also good for lean burgers.

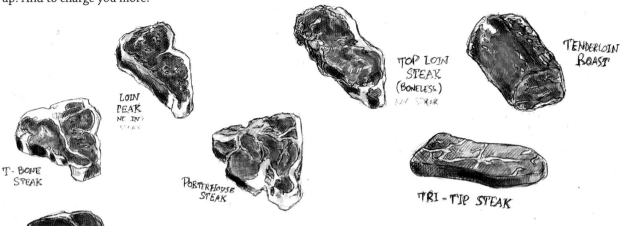

LOIN PEAK NE IN) STEAK

T-BONE STEAK

PORTERHOUSE STEAK

TOP LOIN STEAK (BONELESS) NY STEAK

TENDERLOIN ROAST

TRI-TIP STEAK

TOP SIRLOIN STEAK

Loin: The loin is where the choicest cuts of meat are located. Coming from the cow's fatty area right above the hips, this is where your money steaks are located. The loin is further separated into filet mignon, tenderloin roast, T-bone, porterhouse steaks, strip steak, tri-tip, New York strip, top sirloin, and bottom sirloin. Tender, flavorful, expensive. Like me.

Meat Cuts

Chicken - If you've ever wondered why we refer to cooked cow as beef but cooked chicken (*Gallus gallus*) as chicken, we need to look back about a thousand years ago to when France invaded England. The French conquered the English and ruled over many aspects of the country, including the culinary scene. The effects of this are still seen influencing food terminology to this day. In the ruling-class French dining halls, the English word 'cow' became the French term, *boeuf* [beef]. This is also how the pig became *porc* [pork] and sheep became *mouton* [mutton]. Most people assume that the word 'chicken' escaped this French fate because the lower-class English ate mostly chicken while the French beef-eating rulers overlooked the gamely fowl, but that's a common misconception. Chicken got the French treatment as well and became *poulet* [poultry]. However, this French loanword just didn't stick in English vernacular as 'poultry' was used as an umbrella term that covered all domesticated birds raised for their meat, eggs, or feathers. So, instead of sticking with the confusing blanket terminology, English-speakers just kept calling it chicken and it has become a common protein staple across the globe. **Just remember when you cook chicken, you need to heat it to at least 165°F, 74°C.** No if's, and's, or chicken butts!

BREAST

Breast: This is your big white meat cut of the bird. All of this is pure muscle. There's little fat and little flavor, but this part has good texture and is good in sandwiches, fried, shredded, mixed with salads, baked, marinated, fried again, anything! This is a good hunk of protein; just flavor it how you want. Explains why chickens are so strong and why you shouldn't mess with them. They'll beat you up!

WING

Wing: This is another white meat part of the bird. Lots of connective bits to chew on and some tasty skin, usually fried and covered in sauce.

EGG

LEG   THIGH

Thigh: The upper portion of the leg. Dark meat with a little more fat and flavor than the breast but the coloration can scare off some picky eaters.

Egg: I initially debated listing the egg before the chicken. Chicken eggs are widely used in all sorts of dishes. We could do a whole section on the egg. There are countless ways to eat or prepare them, ranging from eating them raw to burying them in clay for months or even steeping them in tea. Not only has the egg shaped kitchens across the globe, the egg as a cultural symbol has equally spread across the world. Very few foodstuffs have impacted our species as much as the humble egg.

DRUMSTICK

Drumstick: Dark meat from the bottom of the legs. A great, cheap snack and comes with a built-in handle.

Pork- Pork is pig (*Sus scrofa*)! Despite only being domesticated for about half as long as cattle, this little oinker is king in many other ways. Did you know that pig is the most consumed animal on the planet? I didn't; then again, I just ate an entire pack of uncooked hot dogs while writing this page so maybe I'm just in denial. However, despite its popularity, pork isn't a universal food staple and its consumption varies greatly place to place. **When you cook pork, try to cook it to at least medium rare at 145°F, 63°C.** If you want to try something new, try replacing the other meats in our dishes with pork.

LOIN EYE STEAK

LOIN JOINT

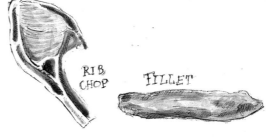

RIB CHOP

FILLET

Pork Loin: This is a choice cut. Lean, tender, boneless, and expensive. This is the piggy equivalent of filet mignon.

Pork Chops: These come from the area near the spine and are part of the loin area. This is the cut for most pork passionate.

LOIN STEAK

SHOULDER STEAK

Pork Butt: This is part of the animal's shoulder. Not sure why it is called the 'butt'. Due to it being part of the tough shoulder area, it will need long, slow cooking. Best when barbecued and slathered in tasty sauce.

BELLY SLICES

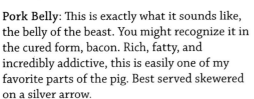

MINI BELLY SLICES

LEG JOINT

Pork Belly: This is exactly what it sounds like, the belly of the beast. You might recognize it in the cured form, bacon. Rich, fatty, and incredibly addictive, this is easily one of my favorite parts of the pig. Best served skewered on a silver arrow.

Ham: A cured cut from the leg of a pig. Originally developed as a way to keep the meat preserved, the various ways of curing the meat have blossomed into a myriad of different varieties and flavors.

Meat often takes center stage in dishes but it is important to remember that not everyone eats meat and there's something to be said for that. Often times vegetarian and vegan options are delicious and are worth trying. I really urge you to eat a black bean burger or enjoy some tofu. Everyone's palette is different but when you start to block out options because some people would list them as a "meat substitute", all you're really doing is limiting your own experience. I'm not going to force you to try something outside your norm, but I will encourage you to be courageous. Go on an adventure outside your comfort zone and see what treasure you find.

Tackle Box Tips

Fish - Fish are an excellent source of tasty protein and excellent fats with lots of flavor potential, but they sadly remain a largely unexplored staple in most kitchens. There are a few small nuisances to cooking fish and other seafood that seem to keep people from diving in headfirst.

Firstly, fish goes bad. All meat spoils but fish has a special, notorious reputation for expiring and getting that distinct "fishy smell". Never buy fish that smells fishy. Only buy fresh fish; fresh fish smells like where it came from, the ocean. There's also nothing wrong with buying frozen fish, just visually inspect it to make sure it isn't dried out or has any obvious flaws. Your best bet is locally sourced fish; the closer the source, the better.

Secondly, how do we eat fish? When you go to the store and go to the fishmonger's counter, what do you see? You see bright red steaks, plucked chicken breasts, and fresh pork chops lined up and ready to take home. You also see whole fish, fish with all the scales, eyes, fins, and everything else that comes on a fish! A lot of people just don't know how to go about preparing a fish and turning it into a tasty filet on a plate. To make things worse, fish are covered with pesky scales that get everywhere and have flesh riddled with small needle-like bones called pin bones. Ok, technically, they aren't even bones, they're calcified nerve endings. That's a fun piece of trivia but it doesn't make me want to eat salmon! There is a learning curve to prepping fish but it is worth it. Nowadays, there are also a lot of options for already prepared fish filets. Start with that. You'll like what you taste and you'll want more.

Thirdly, most people can't tell a salmon from a snapper. There are over 30,000 different types of fish in the ocean. Luckily your supermarket probably only carries a handful of common species. Read the price tags and become familiar with the salmon's pink color, the snapper's red body, the thick steak of a swordfish, and so on. This cookbook is just a starting point. Take your own culinary adventure off these pages and into your life; try new things that we haven't even begun to talk about. You can't go wrong with just asking your fishmonger for help and ideas for a new dish, or talking to your friends or your family. I'm sure someone you know has a great recipe waiting they're just dying to share with you. I know we have a few in our book. We hope you try them out.

Finally, you've sized up your catch, now how do we reel them in? There are many different ways to cook fish. You can boil it, broil it, grill it, fry it or even eat it raw (if it is fresh and clean). Each type of fish is different so do your research, check for pin bones, scrape off the scales, and make sure your fish is fresh. This is your kitchen, take charge and cook up that fish the way you want it.

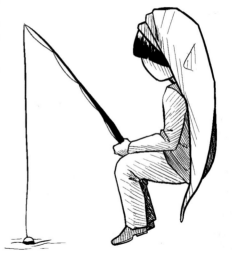

Herbs and Spices

Spices are nice! So are herbs. Experiment in your kitchen but I suggest that you follow your nose when it comes to seasonings. A good rule of thumb is that if it smells good, it tastes good! This does not apply to candles. Let your nose decide if you want to add an extra spoonful of cinnamon but remember, you can always add more but can never take it back out. Not every spice used in this cookbook is listed here but here are some of the more common ones!

Cloves: A spice with a strong, sweet, and almost bitter flavor. Has some heat as well and pairs well with meat, pies, and even fruit.

Cinnamon: Bark with a very strong, spicy flavor. Very aromatic and pairs well with both sweet and spicy. You could say its bark is as big as its bite.

Cumin: A spice with an earthy, warm flavor. Often included in chilis and stews.

Allspice: A spice that tastes like the combined flavor of cinnamon, nutmeg, and cloves. All the spices.

Saffron: An incredibly rare and expensive spice that adds a sweet, almost floral taste. Makes sense since it comes from flowers.

Oregano: An herb with a strong, pungent smell and an earthy, dry taste. There are notes of hay and mint.

Garlic: An herb with an incredibly strong smell that's pungent and spicy. You can taste it with your nose. Goes well with almost everything. I love it.

Rosemary: A unique herb with a strong, aromatic taste of lemon and mint. Also has a hint of heat and tastes great with bread.

Turmeric: Brightly orange, this spice has a pungent and bitter taste.

Basil: An herb with a strong, pungent, often sweet smell. Pairs well with savory cheeses.

Ginger: This is a wonder spice that's underutilized in most kitchens. There are warm, spicy notes that pair well with sweet and savory. A great spice.

Bay Leaf: Don't eat this bitter thing, instead steep in water or in your dish to impart a minty, warm flavor and then discard before indulging.

Chili Powder: Spicy, earthy, and a lot of red color. Make things spicy, like chili. Also, it is a powder.

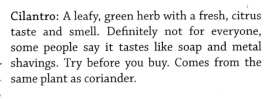

Red Pepper: Hot and spicy, these flakes add a level of complexity with their texture, flavor, and aroma.

Black Pepper: A staple of most tables with its trademark slightly spicy, earthy tones. This now-underappreciated spice can add a lot to a dish. It is important to remember that black pepper is best if it is freshly ground.

Salt: Is this a spice? An herb? Ok, maybe not but it goes here anyways. Salt makes things salty! We all know that but it is a major game changer. It causes a chemical reaction on your taste buds and changes everything. Don't overdo it. Kosher salt is largely just coarse grain salt, similar to Himalayan pink salt, which adds a nice color!

Cilantro: A leafy, green herb with a fresh, citrus taste and smell. Definitely not for everyone, some people say it tastes like soap and metal shavings. Try before you buy. Comes from the same plant as coriander.

Coriander: The dried seeds of the same plant cilantro comes from. This spice has a lot of things going for it, warm, nutty, spicy, earthy!

Cayenne: This is one of the spicier peppers you'll encounter. Great for adding heat to a dish, but use sparingly.

Parsley: This herb often works with other spices to kind of adjust the way you taste. It has a slight bitter taste but pairs well with most things.

Paprika: Mild, sweet, and hot. This is a great spice that people just don't use enough. I put it on everything.

Nutmeg: An intense nutty, earthy spice that can almost be spicy. Use sparingly.

Thyme: This herb has a bright and lemony flavor that pairs well with other spices and herbs.

Kitchen Wisdom

Hey! Listen! Everyone needs some helpful advice so we're here to offer some *Kitchen Wisdom*. These are little tips that you kind of pick up in the kitchen over the course of many courses.

Reheat in the Oven - Far too often do people rely on the microwave to nuke their leftovers. Try a more even and direct heat using an oven next time. Just set it at a low temperature and watch what you're heating. You can always put it back in if you want it warmer.

Keep Your Cookbook Clean - Get a cookbook holder, they're cheap and easy to find online. It will keep this beautiful cookbook clean and help you never lose your page.

A Covered Pot Boils Faster - It is true, a lid can help speed up the process by insulating it.

Best Served Warm on Warm Plates - Wanna up the illusion of a fine meal? Put your plates in the microwave for 30 seconds to warm them up before plating. Little things like this will impress whoever you're cooking for and the food will stay warmer for longer.

Snip Snip Shears - Buy kitchen shears and use them liberally. They are great!

Write in Your Cookbook - Forget what I said about keeping it clean, write in it! Let's be honest, you already got sauce on the thing so you might as well add some notes.

Let There Be Light in Your Pantry - Get a little battery-operated light to stick in your pantry. Who knows what monsters (or missing ingredients) are lurking in the shadows.

Freeze Flat - I always over prepare and have lots of ingredients left over that need to be stored either cold or frozen. I've learned that it is best to take the extra minute or two to make sure they take up as little amount of space as possible.

Cook What You Know for Friends and Family - Got a new recipe you want to try for your parents? Do a test run first, unless it is really simple. You'll never forgive yourself if you accidently bake a friend a birthday cake without any leavening.

Think with Your Tongue - Taste what you're making while you're making it so you can make adjustments to the flavor as you go. Think it could use more salt? Go for it. Cook for your palate.

Watch the Smoke - Some meals will involve some pan searing and sometimes smoke alarms will go off. The absolute worst thing you can do is leave food on the stove while you go to open a door or window. Be mindful of the amount of smoke you're producing while you cook.

Read the Recipes - Do not start cooking until you have read the entire recipe. Often have I had to run to the store or find an ingredient mid-cooking. I have learned the hard way, but I hope you don't have to.

Check Your Eggs - Eggs can and do go bad. Do you know exactly when that carton of eggs in your fridge was purchased? Yeah, I don't know either. You can test if an egg is still good by dropping it in a bowl of cold water. If it sinks, you're good! If it floats, that means gases have built up inside and it should be discarded.

Immerse Yourself in the Immersion Blender - Get one, they're great.

Repeated Recipe Glossary

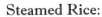

Steamed Rice:
Use a rice cooker but if you don't have that piece of equipment, try this!

Steamed Rice Instructions:
1. Soak the rice in water for 20 minutes and drain off all the water.
2. Add fresh, cool water and gently wash the rice in a circular motion with your hands. Discard the water and repeat 3 to 4 times until the water that drains off is mostly clear.
3. In a large pot, add the rice, then fill with water until the rice is fully submerged and about 1" below the water line. Bring to a boil over medium heat.
4. Once water is boiling, turn heat down to low and cook for 12 minutes or until water is completely absorbed.
5. Remove the plot from heat and set aside, covered, so it can steam for at least 10 minutes.

Pie Crust:
Pie crust is surprisingly versatile. You can use it for a lot of things, like when you want to just make a bunch of pies and eat them. What more could you want?

Pie Crust Ingredients:
-2½ cups Flour
-1¼ cups Vegetable Shortening
-6 tbsp Flour (extra)
-½ cup Cold Water
-1 tsp Salt

Pie Crust Instructions:
1. Use a pastry blender to mix 2½ cups flour and 1¼ cups shortening together in a large bowl.
2. Mix the 6 tbsp flour, ½ cup cold water, and 1 tsp of salt together into a paste in a separate large bowl.
3. Little by little, gently stir the paste into the flour shortening mixture. Add additional paste as it is incorporated, but do not overmix it! Keep it loose and airy so it flakes when baked.
4. Place in the fridge for at least an hour. This yields enough pie crust for three pie bottoms and will keep for several days while refrigerated.

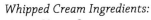

Whipped Cream:
Who doesn't love a nice, sweet dollop of whipped cream on their desserts? Whipped cream is great to add moisture, sweetness, and a touch of lightness to almost any dish.

Whipped Cream Ingredients:
-2 cups Heavy Cream
-½ cup Powdered Sugar
-1½tsp Vanilla Extract (optional)

Whipped Cream Instructions:
1. Place a metal mixing bowl and beaters in the freezer for 15 minutes.
2. Remove the bowl from the freezer. Add the heavy cream, powdered sugar, and vanilla extract (optional for extra flavor) to the bowl.
3. Beat with an electric mixer for 4 to 5 minutes, or until stiff peaks form.

-Li Kovács @LiKovacs

Your Culinary Adventure Begins

Hard Boiled Egg

Start out with something easy! Just boil water!

Ingredients:
- 4 Eggs
- ½ tsp Salt
- Ice Water

Instructions:

1. In a medium pot, add eggs. Add enough water into the pan to cover the eggs with water by 1".
2. Add ½ tsp salt and cover the pot. Set heat to high and bring water to a boil.
3. Once at a full boil, lower heat to medium high and cook for 7 to 8 minutes.
4. Remove the eggs from water and place into a bowl of ice water. Keep the eggs in the ice water until they're cool enough to handle.
5. Crack and peel your high-protein snack.

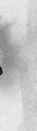

Have you ever wondered why raw egg whites aren't actually white? It turns out the "whites" actually transform into their namesake color after we apply heat. Tiny balls of protein, which are tightly-wound in an uncooked egg, become unwound and begin to tangle up with one another during the heating process. This tangled mess of proteins eventually becomes a jelly-like net that holds its form, unable to unwind itself. Heat isn't the only way to achieve this, though. Whipping raw eggs breaks down the protein bonds in a similar way while also adding air into the mixture. This is how we make a fluffy white meringue.

31

Baked Apples

Ingredients:
- 4 Honeycrisp Apples
- 4 tbsp softened Salted Butter
- ¾ tbsp Ground Cinnamon
- ½ tsp Lemon Zest, freshly grated
- ½ cup Brown Sugar
- 4 Cinnamon Sticks
- 1 tbsp Lemon Juice, freshly squeezed
- ½ cup Apple Juice

Instructions:
1. Preheat oven to 375°F.
2. Wash and partially core apples, leaving enough of the core at the base of the apple (about ½" to 1") to contain the cinnamon plug. We'll get to that in a minute.
3. Mix butter, cinnamon, lemon zest, and brown sugar together in a bowl.
4. Form a plug by shaping the butter and spice mix around a cinnamon stick with your hands. Make sure the plug fits the hole in the apple!
5. Place each plug into the center of each apple.
6. Mix apple juice and lemon juice together in a cast iron skillet. Place the apples upright in the skillet.
7. Put the whole skillet in the oven to bake until apples are soft and the filling is browned, about 1 hour.
8. Eat!

Apples are a type of fruit called a 'pome'. Pomes are easily identiable by their fiberous core with only a few seeds surrounded by edible flesh!

33

Fried Plantains

Ingredients:
- 4 large very ripe Plantains
- ¼ cup Vegetable Oil
- 1 tbsp Vanilla Extract
- 1 tsp Ground Cinnamon
- 1 tsp Salt
- 1 cup White Sugar
- Whipped Cream
- ½ cup Powdered Sugar
- Edible Flower (optional)

A blackened, ripe plantain might look unappealing but that coloration indicates sweetness and sugar content. As the tough starches start to break down into simple sugars, the plantain gets darker and darker.

Instructions:

1. Peel the plantains and cut into halves, lengthwise.
2. Heat a large skillet over medium high heat. Once hot, add ¼ cup vegetable oil.
3. Once oil is hot, lay the plantain halves down in the skillet and drizzle with vanilla extract.
4. Fry until lightly browned and flip, 4 to 7 minutes per side.
5. In a small bowl, mix the ground cinnamon, salt, and white sugar.
6. Drain excess oil by transferring plantains to a paper towel-lined paper plate.
7. Toss the fried plantains in the sugar, salt, and cinnamon mix.
8. Sprinkle powdered sugar over plantains.
9. Carefully place the fried plantains on a plate with whipped cream *(it's in the glossary!)*. Garnish with an optional edible flower.

(Do NOT eat flowers from a bouquet! Unless the flowers are specifically meant for human consumption, most flowers you buy are sprayed with pesticides that can make you sick. Do your research and find something beautiful and delicious.)

Glazed Veggies

Ingredients:
- ½ cup Balsamic Vinegar
- ¼ cup Brown Sugar
- ¼ cup Honey
- 1 lb Carrots, chopped
- ½ lb Green Beans
- 1 lb Small Potatoes, halved
- 1 lb Brussels Sprouts, halved
- 1 Red Onion, sliced
- 2 tbsp Olive Oil
- ¾ tsp Salt
- ½ tsp Black Pepper
- ½ tbsp Sesame Seeds

Instructions:

1. Preheat oven to 425°F.

2. Mix balsamic vinegar, brown sugar, and honey in a saucepan over medium-high heat. Bring to a boil.

3. Reduce heat to low and simmer until reduced by half, about 15 to 20 minutes. The glaze is ready when it can stick to and coat the back of a spoon. *(set aside)*

4. In a bowl toss carrots, green beans, potatoes, brussels sprouts, and sliced red onions. Add olive oil, salt, black pepper, and sesame seeds. Mix well.

5. Transfer vegetables to a foil-lined baking sheet. Roast in the oven until tender and caramelized, about 30 minutes.

6. Place vegetables in a bowl and drizzle with glaze.

Hot Buttered Apple

Ingredients:
-4 Honeycrisp Apples
-2 tsp Cornstarch
-¾ cup Brown Sugar
-¼ cup Butter, cold
-1 tbsp Ground Cinnamon
-½ Cold Water

Toppings:
-Whipped Cream
-1 tbsp Cinnamon
-1 sprig Mint (garnish)
-2 tbsp Salted Butter
 (garnish)

Instructions:

1. Preheat oven to 375°F.

2. Slice 3 of the apples into at least 8 slices each. Partially core the last one, leaving enough of the core at the base of the apple to contain the filling. Set the cored apple aside until step 8.

3. Dissolve cornstarch in ½ cup of cold water and add to oven-safe skillet.

4. Stir brown sugar and half a tablespoon of cinnamon into the cornstarch mixture and bring to a boil over medium heat for 2 minutes, stir occasionally. Reduce heat to low.

5. Add apple slices to skillet. Simmer while stirring constantly until almost tender, about 6 to 7 minutes.

6. Mix cold butter and ½ tbsp of cinnamon together in a bowl until well mixed. Shape the mix into a plug to fill the cored apple.

8. Place cored apple in the middle of the sliced apples in the skillet, hole side up.

9. Bake the entire skillet in the preheated oven for about 15 minutes, until sugar begins to caramelize and apples are tender. *(This is a great time to start working on the whipped cream topping, see the glossary on how to make it.)*

10. Remove skillet from the oven to cool slightly, just enough to handle without burning yourself. *(Should take about as long as it would to finish that fresh whipped cream!)*

11. Place cored apple and sliced apples on a plate. Drizzle both with the glaze from the skillet. Add the whipped cream garnish liberally to the top of cored apple for garnish. Top with the mint sprig, cinnamon, and 2 tbsp of cold butter.

Simmered Fruit

Ingredients:
- ½ cup Light Brown Sugar
- ½ Green Apple
- ½ Red Apple
- ½ Peach
- 5 Strawberries
- 6 oz can Pineapple Juice
- 1 cup Cold Water
- 2 tbsp Orange Zest
- ¼ cup Cold Water (extra)
- 3 tbsp Cornstarch

Garnish:
- Blueberries
- Orange Slice
- Apple Slices
- Strawberries

Instructions:

1. Dice all of the fruit besides what you'll be using for garnish. Toss the diced fruit into a medium pot with 1 cup of cold water, pineapple juice, and orange zest.

2. Boil on medium high heat until the fruit starts to get soft. *(You can check it with a fork; if the fork goes into the fruit with little resistance, it's ready!)* Mix in the light brown sugar and reduce to a simmer over medium low heat. Simmer for about 20 minutes.

3. Once the sugar is completely cooked into the fruit, in a separate bowl, mix 3 tbsp of cornstarch and ¼ cup cold water. Add cornstarch mixture to the fruit and let thicken for 30 minutes over low heat.

4. Pour onto a plate and add additional fruit as a garnish. *(This recipe also functions as a lovely pie filling!)*

You might not be familiar with light brown sugar. Light brown sugar is essentially brown sugar but with less molasses in it, the syrupy stuff that adds the color. I can get into a big diatribe about different sugars and all that but I'll spare you, for now. Mostly, I want you to know that light brown, brown, and dark brown are largely interchangeable and most people won't even notice a difference in flavor. You can even cheat and make your own light brown sugar by adding a little bit of white sugar to brown!

Copious Fried Wild Greens

Strawberry Vinaigrette Ingredients:
-8 oz Strawberries
-2 tbsp Honey
-2 tbsp Apple Cider Vinegar
-3 tbsp Olive Oil
-Salt and Black Pepper
-A pinch of Poppy Seeds

Greens Ingredients:
-12 oz Rainbow Carrots, chopped
(or Orange Carrots)
-1 tbsp Olive Oil
-4 tbsp Butter
-3 Pears
-2 tbsp Honey
-Salt and Black Pepper
-½ cup Chopped Walnuts
-5 oz Arugula
-1 tbsp Balsamic Vinegar
-6 oz Gorgonzola Cheese, crumbled

Instructions:

1. In a food processor or blender, blend all strawberry vinaigrette ingredients. Set aside.

2. Cut carrots into thin, bite-sized pieces.

3. Core and quarter 2 pears, then halve the last pear.

4. In a large pan over medium high heat, add ½ tbsp olive oil and 2 tbsp butter. Swirl to coat the bottom of the pan.

5. Add carrots in a single layer. *(Do not layer them on top of each other.)* Cook without stirring for 5 minutes. Stir carrots, arrange in a single layer, and cook again for 5 to 10 minutes until the carrots soften. Remove carrots from the pan and set aside in a large bowl.

6. Add ½ tbsp olive oil and 2 tbsp butter to the pan; swirl to coat. When the butter is melted, add the pears (flesh side down), honey, salt, and pepper. Cook pears until they are lightly caramelized, about 5 minutes.

7. Add 1 tbsp balsamic vinegar and cook for another minute. Add pears to the bowl with the carrots.

8. Add walnuts, arugula, gorgonzola, and strawberry vinaigrette to the carrot and pear bowl. Toss together until well incorporated and you're looking at a pretty tasty salad.

43

Allspice

Vegetable Omelet

Spicy Ketchup Ingredients:
-2 tbsp Olive Oil
-1 small White Onion, minced
-2 cloves Garlic, minced
-2 Red Habanero, diced thin
-6 oz can Tomato Paste
-2 tsp Salt
-1 tsp Garlic Powder
-1 tsp Onion Powder
-¼ tsp Ground Allspice
-1 tsp Ground Mustard
-½ tsp Smoked Paprika
-1 tsp Red Pepper Flakes
-½ cup Brown Sugar
-12 oz can Crushed Tomatoes
-¼ cup Apple Cider Vinegar

Omelet Ingredients:
-3 large Egg Whites
-2 large Egg Yolks
-2 oz Baby Spinach, chopped
-1 clove Garlic, minced
-Salt and Pepper
-2 tsp olive oil
-2 tbsp Unsalted Butter
-2 tbsp Red Bell Pepper, chopped
-1 tbsp White Onion, chopped
-2 tsp Parmesan, freshly grated
-Tomato (garnish)
-Arugula (garnish)

Ketchup Instructions:
1. Heat oil in a small saucepan over medium-high heat. Add onions and sauté until transparent and brown.
2. Add minced garlic and habaneros, cook until fragrant.
3. Add tomato paste, salt, and spices. Stir until the tomato paste is well mixed with the spices and fragrant.
4. Add in the brown sugar, crushed tomatoes, and vinegar. Stir well. Simmer over low heat until mixture thickens, about 1 hour.
5. Add mixture to a blender and purée.
6. Strain resulting ketchup through a fine mesh strainer into a clean bowl. Cover and set aside.

Omelet Instructions:
7. Crack egg whites into a separate bowl from the egg yolks.
8. Whisk the yolks until homogenous and pale in color.
9. Whisk egg whites until they triple in size with medium peaks.
10. Fold the egg yolks into egg whites until fully incorporated.
11. Add spinach to a frying pan over medium high heat. Cook until it wilts. Add the chopped garlic, salt, and pepper and cook until fragrant. Remove from heat and set aside.
12. Heat 2 tsp olive oil in an 8" nonstick omelet pan over medium high heat. Once the pan is hot, pour in the egg mixture.
13. Cook until bottom of the omelet has set.
14. Lift the sides of the omelette and add butter under the eggs.
15. Add in spinach mix, peppers, and onions over the middle of the eggs and top with parmesan. Jerk the pan to help eggs set a bit better.
16. Cover the pan and cook for another 5 minutes, or until the top of the omelet has set. Fold over onto plate.
17. Top omelet with ketchup and garnish with tomato slices and arugula.

45

Cream of Vegetable Soup

Ingredients:
-2 lbs Leeks,
white and light green part only
-2 lbs Yukon Gold Potatoes, *cubed*
-2 Bay Leaves
-4 large sprigs fresh Thyme
-4 large sprigs fresh Sage
-4 large sprigs fresh Parsley
-Kitchen Twine
-2 Yellow Onions, *chopped*
-4 Carrots, *chopped in rounds*
-4 tbsps Unsalted Butter
-2 cloves Garlic, *minced*
-8 cups Vegetable Stock
-1 tbsp Salt
-1 tsp Black Pepper
-½ cup Heavy Cream

Instructions:
1. First, cut the leeks lengthwise and wash thoroughly to remove any sand and grit. Once washed and dried, thinly slice the leeks crosswise.
2. Create a bouquet garni by tying together the bay leaves, thyme, sage, and parsley with clean kitchen twine.
3. On low heat, melt the unsalted butter in a large pot. Stir in the leeks, carrots, and onions, then cover the pot to let the vegetables sweat for 30 minutes.
4. Increase heat to medium high and toss in the garlic, cooking until fragrant.
5. Add potatoes and stock. Bring to a boil.
6. Once boiling, add the bouquet garni and reduce the heat to low. Cook until potatoes are tender. You can test this by sticking a fork in them.
7. Once tender, remove bouquet garni. Use a hand-immersion blender to blend the soup until smooth. *(A regular blender works fine too if you're in a pinch, but the results can be... a little messy.)*
8. Once smooth, stir in salt, pepper and cream then serve.

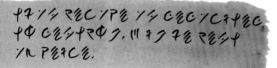

47

Creamy Heart Soup

Ingredients:
- 1 large Seedless Watermelon
- 1 tbsp Vegetable Oil
- 1 Lime, juiced
- 1 Cucumber
- 1 Chili Pepper
- 1 Red Bell Pepper
- ½ Dragon Fruit
- ½ Tomato
- 1 Shallot
- 1 tsp Salt
- ¼ cup fresh Cilantro Leaves
- ¼ cup Half and Half
- 1 tsp Sugar
- ½ cup Radishes
- 1 tbsp Mirin
- Summer Kiss Melon (optional)

Instructions:

1. In a small saucepan on medium high heat, add vegetable oil. Cut the tops and bottoms off of the radishes and thinly slice them. Once the saucepan is hot, add the radishes and sauté until they start to become translucent. *(approximately 5 minutes)*

2. Once they are starting to become soft, add in the mirin. *(**Radishes have a slight peppery, bitter taste to them when they are uncooked. By sautéing them and adding the mirin, the radish will lose some of the bitter taste and become a bit sweeter with the rice wine.**)*

3. Prepare the vegetables. Peel and cut the cucumber into chunks. Core and slice the red bell pepper and chili pepper into small pieces. Dice the tomato half. Mince the shallot.

4. With a spoon, scoop out the dragon fruit. Cut the watermelon in half. *(**If you are going to decorate with the garnishes, cut out a small heart from the watermelon and scoop out a few watermelon balls with a melon baller.**)* Begin to carve half of the watermelon until you get around 4 cups of chopped watermelon.

5. In a blender, add the dragon fruit, cucumbers, peppers, tomatoes, shallot, 4 cups of chopped watermelon, and salt. Blend until smooth.

6. Once smooth, add in cilantro, half and half, sugar, radishes, and lime juice. Blend until smooth and everything is incorporated. *(**This is our gazpacho!**)*

7. With a small strainer, pour the gazpacho into a bowl and strain so you are left with just the liquid and no pulp. Cover the bowl with plastic wrap and chill for 2-3 hours.

8. Hollow out half of the watermelon, cover with plastic wrap and chill. *(**The watermelon bowl is not necessary but it is fun!**)*

9. Once cold, remove from fridge and pour gazpacho inside the watermelon shell to serve. Decorate with melon balls and melon heart garnish. If you want color variety in the melon balls, you can use summer kiss melon balls to garnish as well.

There are two types of commercially available dragon fruit (actually there's more but I don't want to overwhelm you, these are the two COMMON types). The inside of the dragon fruit can be either dark magenta or white, both with small black seeds. We want to use the one with the white flesh for this one since the magenta colored one will change the color of the resulting gazpacho drastically. However, if you end up with the other kind of dragon fruit, don't worry! You'll just end up with an electric pink gazpacho! Also, I have to note, gazpacho might be a bit of a turn off for a lot of people. Because it is a cold soup, this dish might not be a hit with everyone.

Hearty Clam Chowder

Ingredients:
- 3 dozen Hard Shell Clams
- 4 cups Water
- 1 tbsp Unsalted Butter
- 1 large Spanish Onion, diced
- 2 large ribs Celery, cleaned and diced
- Black Pepper
- 2 cups Heavy Cream
- ¼ cup Parsley, chopped
- 5 large Carrots, diced
- ¼ pound Bacon, diced
- 12 Red Potatoes, cubed
- ½ cup Dry White Wine
- 3 sprigs Thyme
- 1 Bay Leaf

ᚢᛏᛏᚲ ᚦᚲ ᚲᛏᛁᚲ
ᚹ/ᛁᚾᚤᛁᚱᚾ/ᚢᚤᛏᛥ.

Instructions:
1. Put the clams in a large, heavy dutch oven, add about 4 cups of water, then set over medium high heat. Cover and cook until clams have opened, approximately 10 to 15 minutes. *(Clams that don't open within that time should be discarded because they've probably gone bad.)*

2. Strain the leftover clam broth through a sieve or through a cheesecloth *(if you're in a pinch, paper towels work also)* and keep it for later. Remove clam flesh from the shell and set meat aside.

3. Wash the dutch oven, return it back to the stove. Add butter, and turn heat to medium low. Add bacon and cook, stirring occasionally until it starts to brown. This should take 5 to 7 minutes.

4. Remove bacon from the pot and set aside. *(Leave in the fond! Fond is the French term for "base" which is best described as the browned and caramelized bits stuck to the bottom of a pan after sautéing or roasting.)*

5. In the dutch oven, add celery, onion and carrots. Cook until they soften. Stir in the potatoes and wine. Continue cooking until the wine has mostly evaporated and the potatoes start to soften.

6. Add in the clam broth, enough that it covers the potatoes in the pot (around 3 cups) then add the thyme, parsley and bay leaf. Partly cover the pot and simmer gently until potatoes are tender, approximately 10 to 15 minutes.

7. At this time, chop the clam meat into bite-sized bits.

8. Once the potatoes are tender, add in the chopped clams, the bacon you set aside, cream, and pepper to taste. Bring to a simmer and remove from heat. Remove the thyme sprigs and bay leaf.

9. Let chowder sit and cure off heat for one hour, reheat to a bare simmer before serving.

Meat Stew

Ingredients:

- ¼ cup All-purpose Flour
- ¼ tsp Black Pepper, freshly ground
- 1 tsp Garlic Powder
- 1 lb Cubed Beef
- 5 tsp Vegetable Oil
- 2 tsp Salt
- 2 tbsp Red Wine Vinegar
- 1 cup Red Wine
- 4 cups Beef Broth
- 2 Bay Leaves
- 1 Onion, chopped
- 5 Carrots, cubed
- 2 cups Peas
- 2 large Potatoes, cubed
- 2 tbsp Tomato Paste
- 1 tbsp Herbes de Provence
- 3 sprigs Thyme

Instructions:

1. Combine flour, pepper, and garlic powder in a bowl. Add the cubed beef and toss to coat well.
2. Heat 3 teaspoons of the oil in a large pot. As it is heating, be sure to add a few pieces of beef at a time; do not overcrowd the pot! Keeping the pieces too close to each other will prevent it from cooking evenly.
3. Cook the beef, turning the pieces until the cubes are browned on all sides, about 5 minutes per batch.
4. After browning the beef, sauté the onions in the pot until translucent.
5. Add 2 tablespoons of tomato paste and 1 tbsp of herbes de provence.
6. Deglaze the pot with the wine and vinegar.
7. Add the herbs, thyme sprigs, and bay leaves.
8. Add the beef broth and bring to a boil, then reduce to a slow simmer. Cover and cook for about 1½ hours. Add carrots and potatoes and cook till tender, this should take around 30 minutes.
9. Finish with two cups of peas 2 to 3 minutes before serving, making sure to remove the sprigs of thyme and bay leaves before you serve.

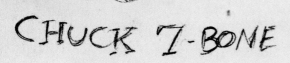

CHUCK 7-BONE

Curry Pilaf

Ingredients:
- 1 medium Onion, chopped
- 1 clove Garlic, finely chopped
- 2 cups Long Grain Rice
- ½ cup Frozen Peas
- 1½ tsp Salt
- ¼ tsp Black Pepper
- ¼ cup Golden Raisins
- 2 tbsp Unsalted Butter
- 2 large Carrots, finely diced
- 2 Eggs
- 2 tsp Curry Powder
- ⅔ cup Water
- ⅔ cup Chicken Stock (or Vegetable Stock)
- 1 strip Orange Zest
- ⅓ cup Cilantro, chopped
- ½ cup Almond

Instructions:
1. Melt butter in a medium sized saucepan over medium heat. Add garlic, onions, carrots, salt, and pepper. Reduce heat to low and cook 2 to 3 minutes until onion is translucent.
2. Increase heat to high and add rice, curry powder, peas, and orange zest. Cook for 2 to 3 minutes, stirring frequently.
3. Add water, stock, and bay leaf. Cover, reduce heat to low and cook for 18 to 20 minutes.
4. Remove from heat and keep covered
5. Scramble eggs in a small oiled pan over medium heat. Separate eggs into small bits.
6. Remove the cover for the rice mix. Fluff and scramble with a fork, remove zest, and bay leaf.
7. Gently toss with a fork and mix in raisins, cilantro, scrambled eggs, and almonds.
8. Serve!

Pilaf is an ancient dish with a history that predates written records. Rice has been a staple grain for over 10,000 years. A pilaf is a simple dish of seasoned rice, often with a meat stock. It is easy to see how such an uncomplicated, almost boring, meal could be relic of the past but can still be enjoyed today.

Fried Egg and Rice

Ingredients:
- 1 cup Short Grain Asian Rice
- 2 large Eggs
- 1 tsp Herbes de Provence
- 1 tsp Olive Oil
- 2 oz Arugula or Romaine
- Salt and Pepper to taste

Instructions:

1. Use our steamed rice recipe in the glossary to prepare the rice.
2. Heat oil in a medium nonstick skillet over low heat until it starts to smoke.
3. Crack 2 eggs into the skillet but try not to let them run together.
4. Cover pan and cook 2 to 3 minutes. *(I like to cook it until the whites are completely set but the yolks are still runny, but you do you!)*
5. On the plate, season arugula or romaine with olive oil, salt, and pepper. Place rice over the greens and then top with an egg.
6. Season egg with salt, fresh ground black pepper, and herbes de Provence to taste.
7. Consume your delicious meal!

FRESH CRACKED BLACK PEPPER
AND GROUND PEPPER
COMBO TASTE THE SAME.
USE YOUR GRINDER!

Too much sodium can be bad for you. This recipe, like several others, is described as salt and pepper to taste. This means add as much salt and pepper as you'd like based on your taste. Pepper has a lot of flavor, but not so much salt. Try to define the taste of salt without using the word 'salt'. Pretty difficult. That's cause salt is just a chemical, a basic one of two different elements. Yet we add it to everything, sweet things, spicy things, savory things, salty things! There's a lot of theories as to why we use it so much but one prevailing one is that we like salt so much because it takes water out of the flavor equation. Think about it, water dilutes things, even flavors. If you use something that sucks up water, you stop the dilution and get more flavor! Think about it the next time you dip some salted fries in a milkshake. What are you tasting?

Crab Omelet with Rice

Ingredients:
-1 cup Short Grain Asian Rice
-3 large Egg Whites
-2 large Egg Yolks
-4 tbsp Unsalted Butter
-1 clove Garlic, minced
-2 tbsp Red Bell Pepper, chopped
-3 oz Lump Crab Meat
-1 fresh Shiitake Mushroom, chopped
-2 Scallions, chopped
-2 tbp Olive Oil

Sauce Ingredients:
-2 cups Chicken Stock
-2 tbsp Cooking Sake
-2 tbsp Cornstarch
-2 tbsp Cold Water
-1 tsp Sesame Oil
-2 tbsp Soy Sauce
-2 tbsp Rice Vinegar
-8 oz can of Green Peas

Instructions:
1. *Use our steamed rice recipe in the glossary to prepare the rice.*
2. Mix cold water and cornstarch together until it becomes a paste-like consistency.
3. Combine remaining sauce ingredients in a pot and bring to a boil over medium high heat. Add cornstarch mixture and cook until sauce has thickened. Mix well.
4. Crack eggs and separate the yolks from the whites into 2 separate bowls.
5. Whisk yolks until homogenous and pale in color.
6. Whisk egg whites until they triple in size with medium peaks. Fold egg yolks into whites. Add chopped mushrooms and scallions and continue folding until fully incorporated.
7. In a frying pan, add chopped garlic, crab meat, and chopped red bell peppers. Cook 3 minutes or until fragrant and set aside.
8. Heat 2 tsp of olive oil in an 8" nonstick omelet pan over medium high heat. Once the pan is hot, pour in egg mixture.
9. Cook until the bottom of the omelet has set.
10. Lift the sides of the omelet and add extra butter under the eggs. Add garlic, crab meat, and pepper mix.
11. Jerk the pan to help eggs set a bit better. This is an art, if you mess up your first couple of omelets, that's ok! Mistake omelets taste just as good, *usually*.
12. Cover the pan and cook for another 5 minutes, or until the top of the omelet has set.
13. Plate rice and lay omelet on top. Fold omelet and pour sauce over. Top with extra crab meat if you have any left!

Meaty Rice Balls

Ingredients:
- 2 cups Short Grain Rice
- Salt
- ¼ cup Brown Sugar, packed
- ¼ cup Reduced Sodium Soy Sauce
- 2 tsp Sesame Oil
- ½ tsp Red Pepper Flakes
- ¼ tsp Ground Ginger
- 1 tbsp Olive Oil
- 3 cloves Garlic, minced
- 1 lb Ground Beef
- 10 slices Prosciutto

If you want to try something more exotic wrap with culatello!

Instructions:
1. Use our steamed rice recipe in the glossary to prepare the rice.
2. In a large bowl, mix the soy sauce, brown sugar, sesame oil, red pepper flakes, and ground ginger.
3. Heat a pan on medium heat and add olive oil. Once hot, add garlic and cook until fragrant and lightly browned.
4. Add ground beef and break it up with a wooden spoon. Once the meat is brown, add the soy sauce mixture and stir well. Simmer for 2 minutes.
5. Dip your hands in water and rub salt on them to prevent the rice from sticking to your hands.
6. Assemble the rice on a plate into a pyramid shape. Poke a hole in the middle with your finger and add a spoonful of meat inside. Seal the hole up with rice and form it into a rice ball shape.
7. Wrap with prosciutto.
8. Enjoy.

61

Mushroom Risotto

Ingredients:
- ⅓ package Dried Porcini
- 4 tbsp Unsalted Butter
- 4 oz Shiitake Mushrooms, stemmed and sliced (or 8 oz Button Mushrooms)
- ¼ cup Light Cream
- Salt and Black Pepper
- 1 tbsp Parsley, chopped
- ⅓ cup Parmesan Cheese, grated
- 4 cups Vegetable Broth (or Chicken Broth)
- ½ cup Dry White Wine
- 1 tbsp Olive Oil
- ⅓ cup Onions, minced
- 1½ cups Arborio Rice
- 1 cup Water
- Basil (garnish)

Instructions:
1. Bring 1 cup of water to a boil. Place the dried porcini in a medium bowl and pour in the boiling water. Let stand for 30 minutes.
2. Strain the porcini liquid into a saucepan with the broth. Place the porcini to the side.
3. Bring the broth to a simmer.
4. Melt 2 tbsp of butter in a skillet. Once it starts to foam, add the fresh mushrooms and cook until soft, 3 to 5 minutes.
5. Chop the porcini and add it to the skillet. Cook for 2 more minutes.
6. Add in cream (reserving 1 tbsp), reduce heat, and let simmer until the liquid is slightly reduced and starts to thicken. Add salt and pepper to taste and set aside off the heat.
7. Heat the rest of the butter and 1 tbsp of olive oil in a heavy pot over medium heat. Add onions and saute until soft, 1 to 2 minutes. (*Do not let them brown.*)
8. Add the rice and stir with a spoon until the grains of rice are nicely coated with oil, butter, and onion.
9. Add the wine and stir until the rice absorbs it.
10. Slowly add in the simmering broth ½ cup at a time. Stir frequently. Do not add the next bit of broth until the previous addition is absorbed. Reserve about a quarter of the broth until the end (a little over a cup).
11. After 18 minutes of cooking and stirring, the rice should be tender. Add the last reserved portion of broth, the reserved cream, the parmesan, and the parsley. Stir vigorously to combine with rice. Garnish with basil and serve immediately.

Vegetable Risotto

Ingredients:
- 3 large Carrots, peeled and diced
- 2 tbsp Unsalted Butter
- ¼ cup fresh Basil
- ¼ cup Light Cream
- 1 tsp fresh Thyme
- 2 cloves Garlic, minced
- Salt and Black Pepper
- A pinch of Sugar
- 1½ lbs small Zucchini, chunked
- 1 lb Tomatoes, grated
- 1 tbsp Parsley, chopped
- ⅓ cup Parmesan Cheese, grated
- 4 cups Vegetable or Chicken Broth
- ½ cup Dry White Wine
- ⅓ cup Onions, minced
- 1½ cups Arborio Rice
- Basil (garnish)

Instructions:
1. Put your broth into a saucepan and bring it to a simmer over low heat.
2. Melt 2 tbsp of butter in a separate skillet. Once it starts to foam, add the onion, zucchini, and carrots with a generous pinch of salt. Cook until soft, 3 to 5 minutes.
3. Add the rice and garlic. Cook, stirring, until the rice grains begin to crackle. Stir in grated tomatoes, sugar, thyme, and salt to taste. Stir often, until the tomatoes reduce slightly and completely coat the rice, 5 to 10 minutes.
4. Add wine and stir until the rice absorbs the wine.
5. Slowly add in the simmering broth, half a cup at a time. Stir frequently. Do not add the next portion of broth until the previous portion of broth is absorbed. Reserve about a quarter of the broth till the end.
6. After 18 minutes of cooking and stirring, the rice should be tender but still a bit firm. Add the reserved broth, cream, parmesan, basil and parsley. Stir vigorously to combine with rice. Serve immediately with basil on top. Garnish with carrots and zucchini.

Veggie Rice Balls

Ingredients:
- 1 cup Short Grain Brown Rice (or Brown Sushi Rice)
- 1 tbsp Black Sesame Seeds
- 1 tbsp Mayonnaise
- 1 tbsp Soy Sauce
- 3 tbsp Chives, minced
- 1 tbsp Wild Rice (or Black Rice)
- 1 Avocado (garnish)
- 1 Sweet Potato
- 2 tsp Lemon Juice

Instructions:

1. Preheat oven to 425°. On a baking sheet, prick sweet potato all over with a fork. Bake until tender, 45 to 50 minutes.

2. Once baked, cut sweet potato into chunks and set aside.

3. Soak both the wild rice and short grain rice in water for 20 minutes then drain off all the water.

4. Use our steamed rice recipe in the glossary to prepare the rice.

5. Add the minced chives, lemon juice, sesame seeds and a few pieces of sweet potato and mix well with the rice.

6. Form the rice ball in your hand with sweet potato, avocado, and mayonnaise in the middle of the rice ball.

7. Top with sesame seeds, soy sauce, and a small piece of avocado.

8. Eat your vegetables!

Dubious Food

Pesto Ingredients:
-2 cups fresh Basil Leaves
-2 tbsp Pine Nuts
-2 cloves Garlic
-½ cup Extra Virgin Olive Oil
-½ cup freshly grated Parmesan

Pesto Instructions:
1. Add basil, pine nuts, and garlic to a blender or food processor. Mix in olive oil as you blend a little bit at a time.
2. Once smooth, add in the cheese and blend slightly, just enough for the cheese to combine with the pesto.
3. Keep refrigerated until chicken is ready.

Chicken Ingredients:
-8 Chicken Drumsticks
-Salt and Black Pepper
-1 tbsp whole Black Peppercorns
-6 sprigs Parsley
-1 Bay Leaf
-3 sprigs Thyme
-Kitchen Twine
-2 bottles Red Wine
-1 cup of Red Wine (extra)
-1 Onion, chopped
-1 Carrot, chopped
-1 Celery Rib, chopped
-4 cloves Garlic, minced
-2 tbsp Flour
-2 tbsp Olive oil
-1 tbsp Butter

Chicken Instructions:
4. Crush and mince garlic. Chop onion, celery, and carrots into large chunks and place them in a large bowl.
5. Pat the drumsticks dry and add them in the bowl with the vegetables. Toss everything together.
6. Tie the parsley, bay leaf, and thyme together with kitchen twine to make a bouquet garni. Add the bouquet garni and whole black peppercorns to the bowl.
7. Add in the red wine and stir, making sure chicken is completely submerged in the wine.
8. Cover with plastic wrap and refrigerate for at least 2 hours and up to 24 hours.
9. Remove chicken from marinade, pat dry, and place to the side. Strain the marinade to separate the vegetables and bouquet garni from the wine and set aside.
10. Season the chicken with salt and pepper to taste.
11. Melt butter in a large dutch oven pot on medium high heat. Once it starts to smoke and brown, add in the olive oil.
12. Add in 2-3 pieces of chicken at a time and sear the sides of the chicken until it's slightly golden brown.
13. Add vegetables and cook until they start to brown, 3 to 5 minutes.
14. Sprinkle flour over vegetables and stir to coat. Add wine marinade and bouquet garni. Cover, reduce heat to low and let simmer for 1½ hours.
15. Once the chicken is tender and cooked, remove the chicken and vegetables from pot.
16. Plate the chicken on a bed of vegetables. Top off with a hearty scoop of pesto. *(It looks very dubious, but very delicious.)*

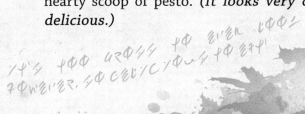

Energizing Glazed Meat

Ingredients:
- 2 8 oz Filet Mignon Steaks
- 4 strips Bacon
- Salt and Black Pepper
- ¼ cup Honey
- 2 cloves Garlic, minced
- ½ cup Balsamic Vinegar
- ¼ cup Brown Sugar
- 1 tsp Ground Ginger
- 1 tsp Dijon Mustard
- 1 tbsp Olive Oil
- 2 tbsp Salted Butter
- Scallions (garnish)
- Toothpicks

Instructions:
1. Preheat oven to 375°F.
2. Mix balsamic vinegar with brown sugar, honey, ginger, and mustard in a medium saucepan over medium heat. Stir constantly until sugar has dissolved.
3. Bring to a boil, reduce heat to low, and simmer until reduced by half, about 15 to 20 minutes. The glaze should coat the back of a spoon.
4. Rest meat until it reaches room temperature. Wrap the sides of the filet mignon with bacon and secure with toothpicks. Season both sides with salt and pepper to taste.
5. In a cast iron skillet over medium high heat, add oil and garlic. Once garlic is fragrant, place the steaks bacon-side down. Cook bacon on all sides, about 1 minute per side.
6. Sear the top and bottom of the filet mignon for 2 to 3 minutes per side or until nice and browned in the cast iron skillet using the bacon fat.
7. Put 1 tbsp of butter on top of each steak and bake for 7 to 8 minutes.
8. Remove and let rest for a few minutes. Pour on all the glaze your arteries can handle. Garnish with some scallions. *(Make sure to completely remove the toothpicks before eating! They are not tasty and you might even choke if you try to eat them.)*

ห7ู ว/นน ห'/ใน
?/ง/ะ ?นา/น.

71

Gourmet Spiced Meat Skewer

Ingredients:
- 1½ lbs Top Sirloin Steak
- 2 tbsp Ground Ginger
- 2 tbsp Curry Powder
- 2 cloves Garlic, minced
- 1 tbsp Garam Masala
- ¼ cup Cilantro, finely chopped
- 1 tsp Ground Coriander
- ½ tsp Ground Cumin
- ½ tsp Ground Turmeric
- ¼ tsp Ground Allspice
- 1 tsp Salt
- 1 tsp Ground Cayenne
- ¼ cup Honey
- 1 cup Plain Yogurt

Instructions:

1. Cut the sirloin steak into roughly 1½" cubes.
2. In a large mixing bowl, add the yogurt, honey, and all of the spices. Mix well.
3. Add in the cubed meat. Mix well, cover and marinate in the refrigerator for at least 30 minutes (or overnight).
4. Add the meat to wooden or metal skewers *(flat ones work best as the meat won't spin)* designed for grilling and gently press with a paper towel to remove any excess marinade.
5. Preheat grill to medium high. Once hot, grill kabobs 4 to 5 minutes per side for medium rare. Adjust to desired doneness. *(Ask your guests how they like their steak.)* Let rest for 10 minutes before serving.
6. Don't eat the skewer.

Tough Meat Stuffed Pumpkin

Ingredients:
- 1 Whole Pumpkin
- 1 lb 90/10 Lean Ground Beef
- Olive Oil
- 1 Yellow Bell Pepper, diced
- 1 Green Bell Pepper, diced
- 1 Orange Bell Pepper, diced
- ½ tsp Ground Cumin
- 1 tsp Salt
- 1 tbsp Pepper
- 2 tbsp Tomato Paste
- 3 cloves Garlic, minced
- 1 cup Tomato Sauce
- 1/4 cup White Cooking Wine
- A pinch of Ground Cloves
- A pinch of Ground Nutmeg
- 1 tbsp Red Wine Vinegar
- ¼ cup Pimiento-Stuffed Green Olives
- 1 tbsp Capers
- 1 tbsp Sherry Vinegar
- ½ large Yellow Onion

Instructions:
1. Preheat oven to 350°F.
2. Cut off the top of the pumpkin. Gut it while separating the seeds and flesh into two different bowls. Bake the pumpkin until it softens, about 15 minutes. Set aside.
3. Heat a small amount of oil in a 10" skillet over medium heat. Add onions, peppers, and garlic. Cook until soft, about 2 minutes.
4. Add cumin, salt, and pepper. Cook until onions are translucent, about 6 minutes.
5. Add tomato paste and cook until incorporated, about 1 minute.
6. Raise heat to high and add the meat. Break it up with a wooden spoon and mix with veggies.
7. Once the meat is brown, add tomato sauce, wine, red wine vinegar, olives, ground cloves, nutmeg, and capers.
8. Cover, reduce the heat to low and simmer until hot, 15 to 20 minutes. Add a splash of sherry vinegar after 5 minutes and taste. Sherry vinegar will add a bit of sweetness. Add more to taste after another 5 minutes if desired. *(Optional: Add some of the pumpkin flesh to the meat for extra pumpkin flavor.)*
9. Fill the baked pumpkin with the meat and bake the whole thing at 280°F for 30 minutes.

(Optional: Place seeds on a baking pan and drizzle a bit of oil and salt on them. Add them to the oven and toast for 15 minutes. Sprinkle on top of the meat after the whole thing is baked.)

Meat and Mushroom Skewer

Ingredients:
- 1 lb Sirloin Beef
- 8 oz whole fresh Mushrooms
- 2 tbsp fresh Rosemary Leaves
- 2 cloves Garlic, minced
- 1 tbsp Brown Sugar
- ½ cup Honey
- 2 tsp Paprika
- 4 tbsp Soy Sauce
- 3 tbsp Vegetable Oil
- 2 tbsp Apple Cider Vinegar
- Salt and Black Pepper

Instructions:

1. Cut the beef into roughly 1" cubes.
2. In a large mixing bowl, combine brown sugar, honey, soy sauce, vegetable oil, apple cider vinegar, garlic, paprika, and rosemary. Mix well.
3. Add cubed meat, making sure to coat well. Cover and marinate in the refrigerator for at least 30 minutes. *(Tastes best if marinated overnight!)*
4. Using grill-safe skewers *(flat ones work best)*, skewer the cubed meat and whole mushrooms, leaving a little space between each piece. Brush the mushrooms with marinade and add salt and pepper to taste.
5. Preheat grill to medium high heat. Once hot, grill kabobs 4 to 5 minutes per side for medium-rare. Adjust to desired doneness *(ask your guests how they like their steak)*. Let rest 10 minutes before serving.
6. Don't eat the stick!

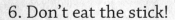

Meat and Rice Bowl

Ingredients:
- 1 lb Top Sirloin Steak, thinly sliced
- ½ cup Low Sodium Soy Sauce
- 1 tbsp Toasted Sesame Oil
- ¼ cup Mirin
- 1 tbsp fresh Ginger, minced
- 3 cloves Garlic, minced
- 2 tbsp Brown Sugar
- 2 tbsp Chili Paste
- 3 Scallions (garnish)
- Pickled Red Onions (garnish)
- 1 tsp Vegetable Oil
- 1 tsp Sesame Seeds
- 1 cup Short Grain Asian Rice

Instructions:

1. Use our steamed rice recipe in the glossary to prepare the rice.

2. In a large bowl, mix soy sauce, sesame oil, mirin, ginger, garlic, brown sugar, and chili paste.

3. Add thinly sliced steak making sure to coat well. Refrigerate for at least 1 hour (or overnight).

4. Remove steak from marinade and pat dry to remove excess.

5. In a pan on high heat, add vegetable oil. Once hot, add steak and cook 1 to 2 minutes on each side. *(You want to hear a nice sizzle and see a good golden brown color!)*

6. Add cooked rice to a bowl and top with meat. Garnish with sesame seeds, pickled onions, and scallions.

TOP SIRLOIN STEAK

Meat Pie

Ingredients:
- 1 cup All Purpose Flour
- 1 tsp Baking Powder
- ¼ tsp Salt
- 1 tbsp Sugar
- 2 tbsp Vegetable Shortening, chilled
- 1 tbsp Butter, chilled
- 1 tbsp Dry Sherry
- 2 large Eggs
- Meat Filling from Tough Meat-Stuffed Pumpkin (recipe on page 77)

Instructions:
1. Preheat oven to 375°F.
2. Sift flour with baking powder, salt, and sugar in a large bowl.
3. Make a well in the center of the dry mix. Place the shortening and butter in the well and then add sherry and 1 egg, combine with hands. Knead until the dough is smooth and stiff.
4. Roll dough out on a smooth flour-covered surface to about an ⅛" thickness. Cut out as many 9" circles as you can. *(You can ball up the leftover dough and reroll it out to make even more circles. Sprinkle extra flour on the dough when rolling it out so it won't stick.)*
5. Place about 2 tbsp of the meat filling from the Tough Meat-Stuffed Pumpkin recipe *(this can be found on page 77)* in the middle of a cut dough circle and place a second circle on top, pinching the edges. Use a fork to crimp edges shut.

6. Place pastries on a lightly oiled baking sheet. Crack the second egg in a small bowl and whisk it to make an egg wash. Use a small, clean paintbrush or silicone brush to apply the egg wash to the tops of the meat pies.
7. Bake for 10 to 12 minutes or until golden brown and crispy.
8. Serve with some fried or steamed rice. It's great on its own too!

Meat Curry

Roux Ingredients:
- 1 cup Unsalted Butter
- ¾ cup All-Purpose Flour
- 1 tbsp Curry Powder
- 1 tbsp Garam Masala
- 1 tsp Ground Cayenne
- 1 tsp Mexican Chili Powder (or Regular)
- 1 tsp Japanese 7 Spice (optional)

Curry Ingredients:
- 1 tsp Olive Oil
- 1 Yellow Onion, diced
- 5 Carrots, chopped
- 5 Potatoes, chopped
- 1 Apple, grated
- 1 lb Meat (Chicken, Pork or Beef)
- 1 cup Red Wine (or Water)
- 8 oz Stock (match to your meat of choice)
- 1 tsp Honey
- 1 tsp Ketchup
- 1 tsp Low Sodium Soy Sauce
- 1 tsp Worcestershire sauce
- 1 cup Short Grain Asian Rice

Roux Instructions:
1. Combine all spices in a medium sized bowl.
2. Melt butter over medium high heat in a saucepan.
3. Slowly incorporate flour. Mix well and constantly stir to avoid the roux from burning. Stir constantly until it turns brown, about 5-10 minutes.
4. Add spices and mix vigorously. Remove from heat.

Curry Instructions:
1. *Use our rice recipe in the glossary to make some nice steamed rice!*
2. Add 1 tsp of oil to a pan and heat on medium high heat. Add your onions and cook until caramelized, about 2 to 3 minutes, stirring occasionally.
4. Add in meat of choice. Sauté until meat is lightly browned. *(Be sure it's cooked to your liking but NOT undercooked!)*
5. Add red wine (or water) and continue to sauté for another minute.
6. Add potatoes and carrots and stir, then add in stock *(don't forget to use the same kind of meat and stock!)*. Once boiling, stir in grated apple, ketchup, honey, and roux.
7. Reduce heat to low and simmer. Add soy sauce and Worcestershire sauce. Continue to simmer for 20 minutes, stirring occasionally. Skim and discard fat that rises to the top.
8. Plate the rice, top with curry, and enjoy!

Salt Grilled Meat

DRUMSTICK

Chicken Ingredients:
- 6 Chicken Drumsticks
- ½ Lemon
- ¼ cup Olive Oil
- 2 tsp Garlic Salt
- 2 tsp Onion Powder
- 1 tsp Black Pepper
- 1 tsp Paprika
- 1 tsp Ground Cayenne
- 1 tsp Italian Seasoning

RIB STEAK

Steak Ingredients:
- 8 oz Ribeye Steak
- ½ tbsp Garlic Salt
- ½ tbsp Onion Powder
- Black Pepper
- 2 tbsp Extra Virgin Olive Oil
- ½ tbsp Italian Seasoning
- ½ tbsp Salted Butter
- 2 tsp Pink Salt
- 3 sprigs Thyme
- ½ Lemon

Chicken Instructions:
1. Juice half a lemon in a small bowl. In the same bowl, mix in olive oil, garlic salt, onion powder, Italian seasoning, pepper, paprika, and cayenne.
2. Pour over chicken and seal in a zippered plastic bag. Massage to completely marinade the chicken. Refrigerate for at least 30 minutes. *(Overnight will result in a more tender, juicer chicken!)*
3. Preheat oven to 425°F.
4. Place chicken on a foil-lined baking sheet. Bake, uncovered, for 25 minutes. *(Optional: you can season it with some pink salt.)*
5. After baking the chicken for 25 minutes, flip the drumsticks over and bake another 10 minutes. After they are no longer pink and have an internal temperature of at least 165°F, they are ready to go.
6. Keep the chicken warm while you prepare the steak by covering it with foil and keeping it in the oven, set at the lowest temperature.

Steak Instructions:
7. Rub both sides of the steak with 1 tbsp of olive oil. Season with onion powder, garlic salt, pepper, and Italian seasoning. Rub the seasoning into both sides of the meat.
8. Drop the thyme sprigs on the steak and wrap in plastic wrap until the steak hits room temperature. *(Cooking a steak at room temperature will allow the steak to cook more evenly and quickly!)*
9. Once the steak is at room temperature, sprinkle salt on both sides.
10. In a pan on medium high heat, add butter and remaining olive oil. Add steak to the pan and sear one side, about 2 minutes.
11. Flip steak, lower heat to medium low and cook for 2½ more minutes. Add half a lemon to the pan, cut side down.
12. Remove the steak and transfer to a cutting board. Let rest for 10 minutes.

Assembly Instructions:
13. Remove the chicken from the oven and plate with the steak. Additionally, sprinkle some pink salt if you want some extra texture and saltiness.
14. Squeeze the lemon that was cooked in the pan with the steak on top of the meat. Your dish is ready to be served! Dig in!

Spicy Pepper Steak

Ingredients:

- 12 Habaneros
- 5 cloves Garlic, crushed and peeled
- 1 cup Carrots, chopped and peeled
- 1 Yellow Onion, chopped
- 1 cup White Vinegar
- 1 cup Water
- 1 tsp Salt
- 1 tbsp Ground Cumin
- 1 tbsp Ground Turmeric
- ¼ cup Sugar
- ⅓ cup Lime Juice
- ⅓ cup Orange Juice
- 2 tbsp Olive Oil
- 3 New York Strip Steaks
- 3 Pork Chops
- Salt and Black Pepper
- 2 Habaneros (garnish)
- Mixed Greens (garnish)

Instructions:

1. Remove stems and seeds from habanero peppers.
2. In a pan over medium heat, roast 1 tbsp of olive oil and garlic until very dark.
3. Add habaneros, carrots, onions, vinegar, water, salt, cumin, turmeric, lime juice, orange juice and sugar. Simmer on low heat for 20 minutes until carrots are soft.
4. Place pan contents into a blender or food processor, add in the orange and lime juice and blend until smooth. Set aside to cool.
5. Season steaks and pork chops with salt and black pepper to taste.
6. Once the marinade has cooled, add steak and pork into a bowl and cover with marinade. Cover and refrigerate for at least 3 hours (*preferably overnight*).
7. Heat pan to high heat. Once hot, add 1 tbsp of oil and steaks. Char one side of the steak, reduce heat to medium and continue cooking for 3 minutes. Flip and repeat.
8. Once both sides are done, turn steak to the side and sear the fattiest side on high heat for one minute.
9. Add pork chops to the same pan and heat to medium high. Cook for 4 minutes per side. Remove from heat and set aside to rest.
10. Plate on a bed of mixed greens along with a few extra uncooked habanero peppers as a garnish. 7ΦΨ ꓵLC ϟⱲƐƐ4!

TOP LOIN STEAK (BONELESS)

NY STEAK

Fish Pie

Ingredients:

-1 lb Cod, cubed
-½ lb medium Shrimp, peeled and deveined
-½ cup Butter
-2 Yukon Gold Potatoes, peeled and cubed
-2 small Leeks, chopped
-3 cloved Garlic, minced
-½ cup All-Purpose Flour
-4 cups Milk
-1 cup Carrot, diced
-1 cup Peas, frozen
-2 tsp Salt
-1 cup Celery, chopped
-½ cup Mushrooms, sliced
-4 large sprigs fresh Thyme
-4 large sprigs fresh Sage
-4 large sprigs fresh Parsley
-Kitchen Twine
-1 tsp Black Pepper, freshly ground
-1 large Egg
-Pie Crust

Instructions:

1. Melt butter over medium high heat in a large Dutch oven. Add in potatoes, leeks, celery, and mushrooms and sauté for 10 minutes.

2. Tie the thyme, sage, and parsley with kitchen twine into a bouquet garni. Add in the garlic and bouquet garni. Stir well till garlic is fragrant, which should be about 1 minute.

3. Sprinkle flour over vegetables and stir constantly for 3 minutes. Whisk in milk and bring to a boil. Reduce heat to low and bring it to a simmer.

4. Add the frozen peas, shrimp, carrots, salt, pepper, and cod. Simmer for 5 minutes then remove the filling from heat.

5. *Use the recipe from our glossary to make a pie crust.* You should have more than enough for this recipe.

6. Roll out pie crust to about ¼" thickness. Cover the sides and bottom of a 9" oval disposable pan. Fill the now covered pan with the filling.

7. Cover the pie with another ¼" thick piece of pie crust. Press down on the edges of the pie pan where the two pieces of crust meet with a fork to seal.

8. You can decorate the top of the pie! Use additional pieces of crust to make it look just like a fish! I added eyes and fins! You can even make flakey scales.

9. Prick a few holes in the crust with a fork to let steam escape from the pie as it bakes.

10. Take the egg and break it into a small bowl. Whisk it to make your egg wash. Brush the top of the pie with egg wash to give it that nice golden shine.

11. Bake at 400°F for 14 to 16 minutes or until pastry is golden brown.

12. Let cool so you don't burn the inside of your mouth when you enjoy it.

Glazed Seafood

Ingredients:
- ½ lb Salmon Fillet
- ⅓ cup Honey
- 1 tbsp Brown Sugar
- 2 tbsp Butter
- ¼ cup Low Sodium Soy Sauce
- 2 tbsp Lemon Juice
- 1 tbsp ground Ginger
- 10 fresh Thyme Leaves
- Salt and Black Pepper
- 2 cloves Garlic, minced
- 2 wedges Lemon (garnish)
- 1 tbsp Olive Oil

Instructions:
1. In a small saucepan on medium high heat, add the butter, brown sugar, and honey. Mix well and cook until small bubbles form. Set aside to cool. This is your honey glaze.

2. As it's cooling, stir in the ginger, lemon juice, and soy sauce. Mix well until everything is incorporated.

3. Take your salmon out of the fridge and make sure you dry it off with a paper towel. If you cook salmon that is damp, the excess moisture will drop the temperature around the wet areas and it will cook unevenly.

4. Cut several deep slits widthwise in the salmon fillet, leaving about a 1" gap between each slit. This will prevent the fish from curling up in the pan. Season the salmon with some salt and pepper, making sure you season inside the grooves that you just cut. After seasoning it, add some thyme leaves to the cuts as well.

5. Heat a saucepan on medium high heat and add 1 tbsp of olive oil. Right before the pan starts to smoke, add your salmon, skin side down. If it no longer has skin, place the side that the skin was on down. We want to make sure the pan is nice and hot before adding the salmon. *(If your pan isn't hot, the salmon will form a chemical bond with the pan and will cause it to stick.)* Once it's in the pan, do not move the fish at all.

6. Cook the salmon for 5 to 6 minutes or until ⅓ of it is cooked. You will see it slowly change color starting with the bottom and slowly making its way up.

7. Glaze the top of the salmon with a bit of the honey glaze. Once glazed, flip the salmon and add garlic to the pan. Cook for 1 minute, until the garlic is fragrant. Season this side of the salmon with some salt and pepper. Once a minute has passed, add the rest of the honey glaze to the pan. Cook until it's reduced a third of the way. This should take 4 to 5 minutes. During this time, make sure you baste the salmon with the glaze in the pan using a spoon. Once fully cooked, remove.

8. Grab a plate and ladle a generous amount of glaze onto it. Place the salmon on top of the glaze and then ladle even more glaze on top. Garnish with additional lemon wedges.

9. Enjoy your glaze (and salmon).

Hearty Salmon Meunière

Salmon Ingredients:
- 2 Salmon Steaks
- 1 tbsp ground Black Pepper
- 1 tbsp Garlic Salt
- 1 tsbp Onion Powder
- 1 large Egg
- ½ cup Wheat Flour
- 3 tbsp Unsalted Butter
- 1 sprig fresh Thyme

Sauce Ingredients:
- 2 cloves Garlic, minced
- ½ cup White Wine
  (or Chicken Stock)
- 1 cup Unsalted Butter
- ⅔ cup Heavy Cream
- 2 tbsp Lemon Juice
- 1 tbsp Flour
- 1 tbsp fresh Dill
- 1 tbsp dried Oregano

Garnish:
- 2 cups Arugula
- 2 fresh Tomatoes

Instructions:

1. Take out salmon from the fridge and pat dry with a paper towel to take out all the moisture. Let salmon sit for 20 minutes to get to room temperature

2. Add wheat flour to one bowl and crack one egg in another bowl. Whisk the egg until scrambled, this is your egg wash.

3. Season the salmon steak with pepper, garlic salt, and onion powder. Rub spices into the salmon. Flip and repeat on the other side.

4. Dip the salmon steak into the egg wash and then coat both sides with wheat flour. Be sure the whole salmon is covered.

5. In a pan, melt the butter on medium heat until it's completely melted and the pan is well coated.

6. *If your salmon steak doesn't have skins on the sides, skip this step. If it does, follow this step and be careful!* Start frying the salmon's skin in the pan. Hold the steak with some sturdy tongs and fry the first side of skin for 1 minute, until it gains a slight crisp. The flip to the skin on the other side and fry for 30 to 45 seconds. Lastly, place it flat side down and fry for an additional minute.

7. Flip the salmon so the last uncooked side is finally face down in the pan for 3 to 4 minutes. Add thyme to the pan. After that, flip to the other flesh side cook for an additional 3 minutes, until the flour and flesh becomes nice and crispy. Remove from heat and set aside.

8. For the sauce, mince two cloves of garlic, then add to it to a separate saucepan over medium high heat. Cook the garlic until it becomes fragrant.

9. Add the white wine (or chicken stock) and bring to a boil. Add in the fresh dill and oregano. Reduce over medium high heat until only about 2 tbsp of liquid remain. Reduce heat to low and whisk in butter, a little bit at a time, until sauce is smooth and all of the butter is incorporated.

10. Whisk in half of the cream and all of the lemon juice. Once smooth, add in flour. Once the flour is well-mixed, add in the last half of the cream until the sauce becomes thick.

11. On a plate, lay down a bed of arugula and garnish with some fresh tomato halves or slices. Lay down the salmon and pour the sauce on top. The Salmon Meunière is done! Dig in!

Fish Skewer

Ingredients:

-½ cup Salt
-1 tsp Rice Wine Vinegar
-½ cup Soy Sauce
-2 tbsp Lemon Juice
-1 tbsp Pineapple Juice
-Old Bay Seasoning
-4 Mackerel or Trout
(or any Small Fish)
-Metal Cooking Grate
-Vegetable Oil
-Aluminum Foil
-Bamboo Skewers (soaked in water overnight)
-A Cozy Fire

Instructions:

1. Combine rice wine vinegar, soy sauce, lemon juice, and pineapple juice in a bowl. Set aside.
2. Pat dry fish with a paper towel. Place the fish on a plate and pack it with salt. Rest at room temperature for 1 hour. (*The salt removes moisture from the flesh by 'sweating' out the fish and intensifying its flavor.*)
3. Get an open fire going with hardwood such as oak, birch or maple to avoid a bitter-tasting fish. (*Especially avoid evergreen wood.*)
4. Rinse off all the salt from the fish with cold water and dry again thoroughly with paper towels.
5. Run a skewer through each fish's mouth and down along its spine and then coat liberally with vegetable oil. Wrap the metal cooking grate with aluminum foil and coat with oil as well.
6. Place the grate about 1" above the flames if you can. Place the fish on the grate and cook until each side's skin is nice and crispy. Use the skewer to help flip the fish and try to cook both sides evenly. Let the fish get to the point where you can see it sizzle and the eyes cloud over, and then cook for at least one minute longer. (*Timing the perfect sear on this will always be difficult over an open flame. Just keep an eye out and make sure they don't burn. I can't give you a good time estimate because so many factors will go into the temperature and cook time; things like wind, humidity, ambient temperature, elevation, and more. You really have to feel it out. Just remember, you can always cook it more but you can't cook it less!*)
7. When fish is cooked and the flesh is white and flaky, remove from heat. Remove from heat. Drizzle the sauce from the beginning of this recipe liberally over the fish. Then drown it in Old Bay seasoning. Enjoy but watch out for pin bones in the flesh.

This recipe is a mixture of traditional skewer cooking over an open flame and Japanese shioyaki. In Japanese, shioyaki roughly translates to "salt grilling". It is a popular manner of cooking fish in Japan even to this day. However, the Japanese usually use a grill, not an open flame and they keep the fish farther away from the heat source. Our recipe will entail a little more char but the addition of our sauce will hopefully keep the meal juicy and flavorful!

Pepper Seafood

Ingredients:
- 1 large whole Snapper Fish, cleaned and gutted
- 6 cloves Garlic, minced
- 2 Habaneros, minced
- 2 tsp Ground Cumin
- 2 tsp Ground Coriander
- 1 medium Red Onion, sliced into rounds
- 2 Red Bell Peppers, sliced into rounds
- 1 tbsp Chili Powder
- ½ tsp Ground Turmeric
- 1 Lemon, sliced thin
- 2 tsp Lemon Juice
- 1 tsp Ground Allspice
- 1 tsp Paprika
- ½ cup Parsley, coarsely chopped
- 2 tsp Thyme, finely chopped
- 3 tbsp Olive Oil
- 2 Habaneros (garnish)

Instructions:

1. Preheat oven to 425°F.

2. Add all the spices (except paprika and parsley), half of the minced garlic, both of the minced habaneros, 1 tbsp oil and 1 tsp of lemon juice to a food processor and blend it into a smooth marinade. Cut 3 slits on both sides of the snapper, from the top to the bottom of the fish. Rub the marinade all over it.

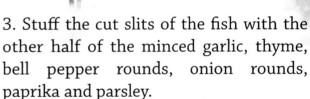

3. Stuff the cut slits of the fish with the other half of the minced garlic, thyme, bell pepper rounds, onion rounds, paprika and parsley.

4. Place the stuffed fish on a lightly oiled baking sheet. Drizzle with remaining olive oil and top the fish with lemon rounds. Roast for 25 minutes until the fish flakes. Remove and drizzle remaining lemon juice on top and garnish with habaneros before serving.

Seafood Fried Rice

Shrimp Ingredients:
-5 large Shrimp raw
-2 tbsp Soybean Oil
-1 tsp Garlic Butter
-1 tbsp Lemon Juice
-Salt and Black Pepper

Rice Ingredients:
-1 cup Medium Grain Rice, uncooked
-1½ tbsp Garlic Butter
-½ cup Yellow Onion, chopped
-½ cup Carrot, chopped
-1 cup Peas, frozen
-3 tbsp Sesame Seeds
-2 large Eggs
-1 tsp Sesame Oil
-1 tbsp Soy Sauce
-Salt and Black Pepper

Instructions:
1. Heat a pan on medium-high heat. Once hot, add the soybean oil then the shrimp. Cook about 3 minutes per side. Add in the garlic butter and cook for an additional 1 to 2 minutes, until shrimp are pink and done.
2. Squeeze lemon juice over the shrimp and add salt and pepper to taste.
3. Remove from heat and set aside.
4. Cook a scrambled egg in a small oiled pan over medium heat.
5. In a large bowl, mix rice, peas, onions, carrots, and scrambled eggs. *(If you aren't using a wok to cook the rice, just use our steamed rice recipe to cook the rice before adding the other ingredients.)*
6. In a wok over medium high heat, add sesame oil. Once it starts smoking, add the garlic butter. When butter starts to melt, add in rice mix.
7. Add soy sauce, salt, pepper, and sesame seeds. Mix well.
8. Cook rice for 6 to 8 minutes, stirring often. Toss in the shrimp in with the fried rice and serve while warm.

Ingredients:
- Olive Oil
- 12 raw Jumbo Shrimp, peeled and deveined
- 8 fresh Mussels, debearded and cleaned
- 2 tbsp Paprika
- 1 tbsp Ground Cayenne
- ¼ cup White Wine
- A pinch of Saffron
- ½ cup Red Bell Pepper, diced
- ¼ cup Green Bell Pepper, diced
- 1 Red Bell Pepper, sliced into rings
- 1 Green Bell Pepper, sliced into rings
- 1 tbsp Ground Cumin
- 2 tbsp fresh Thyme
- 2 Bay Leaves
- ½ Yellow Onion, chopped
- ½ Yellow Onion, sliced into rings
- 3 cloves Garlic, minced
- 4 cups Fish Stock (or Chicken Stock)
- 2 cups Bomba Rice (or Arborio Rice)
- 15 oz can Crushed Tomatoes
- 1 tbsp Lemon Juice
- Salt and Black Pepper

Saffron

Browning the rice will help keep its starchiness, giving it a nice texture that will keep it from becoming mushy. This caramelized bottom layer is called socarrat, which is key to a perfect, traditional paella.

Saffron is the most expensive spice in the world. It's made from the thread-like stigma of the crocus flower. Each flower only has three stigmas and must be harvested by hand. It can be difficult to find as well as expensive as I've mentioned before. Especially due to the fact that the flowers only bloom for one week a year. If you can't find any, don't worry, I can help! A cheap substitute would be to mix ¼ tsp turmeric with ½ tsp paprika. Nothing can beat authentic saffron but the real stuff could drain a giant's wallet!

Seafood Paella

Instructions:
1. In a bowl, toss the shrimp in olive oil, salt, pepper, paprika, and cayenne pepper until they are well-coated. Let the shrimp marinate in the bowl for 15 minutes.
2. Combine lemon juice, saffron, salt, and stock into a pot. Let the saffron soak for 15 minutes then remove the threads. Steeping the saffron rehydrates the threads and improves its flavor. Next, crush the saffron threads with a spoon. Stir them back in and let it sit for another 5 minutes. Then place on low heat.
3. Warm a paella pan on medium high heat. Once hot, add oil and garlic. Cook garlic until fragrant but not browned, about 1 to 2 minutes. Next, add chopped onions and bell peppers. Cook for 3 to 5 minutes, until they are translucent and soft. Add in bell pepper rings and onion rings and cook for another 3 minutes.
4. Add the rice into the paella pan and toast until lightly browned, 2 to 3 minutes. Add the wine. Stir until it is absorbed.
5. Add in the tomatoes, stock, bayleaf, cumin, and thyme. Stir until combined and flatten to a smooth layer. Bring to a simmer, then reduce temperature to low.
6. Nestle the mussels and shrimp into the rice without disturbing the flat rice layer too much. Cook for 10 minutes or until the stock is absorbed by the rice. When almost all of the stock is gone, turn heat up to medium high and cook for 1 minute to burn the rice on the bottom of the pan.
7. Remove the paella from heat and let sit, covered, for 7 to 10 minutes. Uncover the paella, remove the bayleaf, sprinkle some paprika on top, and serve.

Seafood Rice Balls

Ingredients:

- 1 cup Short Grain Asian Rice
- Nori
- 3 tbsp Salted Butter
- 1 lb raw Shrimp, peeled and deveined
- 3 cloves Garlic, minced
- 3 tbsp Lemon Juice
- 2 tsp Paprika
- ½ tsp Onion Powder
- ¼ tsp Black Pepper
- ¼ tsp Cayenne Pepper
- 2 tsp Mayonnaise
- ½ tsp Sea Salt

Instructions:

1. Mix spices and 2 tbsp of lemon juice in a bowl. Set aside.

2. In a large pan over medium high heat, add butter. Once it starts to melt, add garlic. Cook until fragrant and starts to slightly brown. Add shrimp and spice mix, mix well and cook for 4 to 5 minutes. *Cooked shrimp is ready when it curls up and looks like a 'C', overcooked shrimp will roll up completely to make an 'O'.*

3. Set aside to cool once cooked.

4. Once cool, finely mince the shrimp and mix with mayonnaise and 1 tbsp of lemon juice. Set aside some shrimp for garnish.

5. Use the recipe from our glossary to prepare some steamed rice. *(Make sure you have enough!)*

6. Dip your hands in cold water and rub salt on them to prevent the rice from sticking while you prepare the rice balls. Assemble the rice on a plate into a pyramid shape. Poke a hole in the middle with your finger and add a spoonful of shrimp mix inside. Seal the hole with rice and form it into a ball shape.

7. Sprinkle ½ tsp of salt over the rice balls. Add a piece of nori to hold the ball more easily. Top with minced shrimp as a garnish.

Ingredients:

- Pie Crust
- 3½ lbs Apples
- (About 5 Apples)
- 6 tbsp Dark Brown Sugar
- 1 tbsp Lemon Juice
- 2 tbsp All-Purpose Flour
- 1 tsp Lemon Zest
- ½ cup Granulated Sugar
- ¼ tsp Salt
- ½ tsp Ground Cinnamon
- 2 tbsp Cornstarch
- ¼ tsp Ground Nutmeg
- 2 tbsp White Sugar
- 1 large Egg

Instructions:

1. *Make some pie crust using our recipe in the glossary.*
2. Preheat oven to 400°F.
3. Prep the apples by coring, peeling, and slicing them. *(If you don't want to weigh out the apples, just use 5 apples. We recommend Honeycrisp and Granny Smith apples, 3:2 ratio.)*
4. In a bowl, combine apples, lemon zest, lemon juice, granulated sugar, dark brown sugar, salt, cinnamon, and nutmeg. Toss until the sugar is dissolved and the apples are evenly coated. Let sit for at least 30 minutes.
5. Remove apples from the bowl, leaving the syrup that has formed behind. Pour this syrup into a small saucepan.
6. On medium heat, bring the syrup to a boil. Reduce heat to low and simmer until reduced by half.
7. Pour the syrup back over the apples and coat with flour and cornstarch.
8. Put the pie crust into a pie pan and then fill with the apple filling. Add another piece of pie crust on top of the filling and crimp edges with a fork to seal.
9. Cut a few slits in the top crust to allow the steam to escape.
10. Crack your egg in a small bowl and whisk. Use this egg wash to brush the top of the pie. Sprinkle the top of the pie with 2 tbsp white sugar.
11. Bake 15 minutes, then reduce the heat to 350°F. Continue baking until crust is golden brown, about 45 minutes to 1 hour and 15 minutes.
12. Remove from oven and let cool. Enjoy while still warm with some cold milk.

CYC JGw LRGW JGw CHR GJYRC
JGwR GWR CYRRFII GR!

Carrot Cake

Ingredients:
- 2 cups Flour
- 2 tsp Ground Cinnamon
- 1 tsp Baking Powder
- ¼ tsp Salt
- ⅔ cup Butter, softened
- 1 cup Sugar
- 3 large Eggs
- ⅔ cup Milk
- 1 lbs Carrots, grated
- Whipped Cream
- 1 small Carrot (optional)

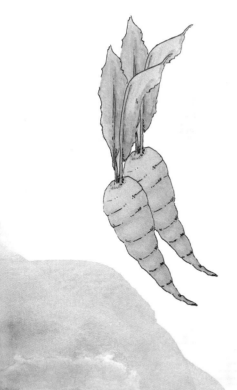

Instructions:

1. Preheat oven to 350°F.

2. Mix flour, cinnamon, baking powder, and salt in a bowl together.

3. In a separate bowl, beat butter and sugar at medium speed until light and fluffy.

4. Mix in the eggs, one at a time, into the butter mix.

5. Lower the speed and alternate between adding a spoonful of the flour mixture and a splash of milk to the butter and egg mixture. Stir in grated carrots.

6. Grease a 9" cake pan and dust it with flour. Pour in the batter and bake for 40 minutes or until you can stick a toothpick in the center and it comes out clean.

7. Transfer to a cooling rack and let cool for 10 minutes. Remove from the pan after 10 minutes to finish cooling.

8. Top each slice with a dollop of fresh whipped cream *(see our glossary for the recipe)* and a small carrot for optional garnish.

Pumpkin Pie

Ingredients:
-15 oz can Pumpkin Purée
-⅔ cup Dark Brown Sugar
-½ tbsp Ground Cinnamon
-1 tsp Ground Ginger
-½ tsp Ground Nutmeg
-¼ tsp Salt
-½ cup Heavy Cream
-1½ cups Half and Half
-3 large Eggs
-2 Egg Whites
-Pie Crust

Instructions:
1. *Make a pie crust using our recipe from the glossary.* You should have more than enough for this recipe.
2. Preheat the oven to 450°F.
3. Roll out pie crust into a ¼" thick sheet and place in a deep, 9" pie plate. Cut off extra crust and store in the fridge for later.
4. Brush egg white onto the the entire crust and chill in the fridge for 1 hour.
5. In a large bowl, mix pumpkin and sugar. Once sugar is incorporated mix in the eggs.
6. Mix in the remaining spices, cream, and half and half. Stir well to blend.
7. Pour filling into the pie crust and bake for 10 minutes.
8. Reduce the temperature to 350°F and bake for an additional 35 to 55 minutes. *(You can tell the pie is ready when you can insert a butter knife into the center of the pie and pull it out. If there's nothing on it when it comes out, your pie is done!)*
9. Once the pie is fully cooked, remove from oven to let pie set and cool.

Egg Pudding

Ingredients:
- 1 cup Sugar
- 3 large Eggs
- 2 large Egg Yolks
- 14 oz can Sweetened Condensed Milk
- 12 oz can Evaporated Milk
- 2 tsp Vanilla Extract
- 3 tbsp Bourbon (or Water)
- ¼ cup Warm Water

Instructions:
1. In a saucepan over medium heat, add sugar. Stir continuously, not every other Twitter post.
2. As soon as the sugar comes to a boil, stop stirring. The sugar should turn into a dark amber caramel, about 2 to 3 minutes.
3. Add warm water and 3 tbsp bourbon (or a little more water). Stir until combined. Remove your caramel sauce from heat and let cool to room temperature.
4. Preheat oven to 325°F
5. In a mixing bowl, whisk to combine the whole eggs, egg yolks, condensed milk, evaporated milk, and vanilla.
6. Divide the custard mixture evenly into 6 oz greased ramekins. Bake for 12 to 15 minutes. Remove and refrigerate for at least 2 hours.
7. When ready to serve, run a small knife around the edge of the ramekin and take custard out. Put on a plate and pour caramel sauce on top.

This unassuming dish goes by a variety of names worldwide, including: flan, purin, rosada, tocino del cielo, dulce de leche, pudim, quesillo, and more. It is commonly flavored with countless ingredients, ranging from lime to passion fruit to rosewater.

Egg Tart

Ingredients:
- Pie Crust
- ½ cup Sugar
- 1 cup Water
- 3 large Eggs
- ⅓ cup Evaporated Milk
- ¼ tsp Vanilla Extract
- A pinch of Salt
- A pinch of Ground Cinnamon

Instructions:

1. *Use our pie crust recipe from the glossary to make the pie crust.* This recipe makes enough filling for 4 tarts. *(You will have a ton of leftover crust, so we suggest for you to halve the initial pie crust recipe, or just do what I do: make more and eat all of it!)*

2. Mix the sugar and a cup of water together in a small pot. Bring to a boil, remove from heat and set the mixture aside to cool to room temperature.

3. Whisk in eggs, evaporated milk, vanilla extract, salt, and cinnamon into the sugar water. Set aside.

4. Press pie crust dough into 4 separate 3" tart tins. Crust should be about 1/4" in thickness. Refrigerate the tins for at least 15 minutes.

6. Preheat the oven to 350°F.

7. Fill the tart shells about ¾ of the way full with custard and place tarts in the oven. Bake for 30 to 40 minutes or until golden brown.

8. Remove from the oven and enjoy warm.

9. Use leftover dough to make more. *(Very important.)*

Despite being a nearly ubiquitous, flavor, vanilla is actualy the second most-expensive spice on the market, behind saffron. This flavoring, derived from a specific genus of orchids, is grown mostly in Madagascar and Indonesia. The long, black seed pods are harvested daily and the work is very labor intense, largely because it is hard to tell when the pods are actually ripe.

Energizing Honey Candy

Ingredients:
- 1 cup Sugar
- ½ cup Honey
- ½ cup Water
- Candy Thermometer

Instructions:

1. In a heavy 2-quart saucepan, combine sugar, water, and honey. Cook over medium heat, stirring constantly, until the sugar and honey have dissolved.

2. Insert candy thermometer. Continue stirring gently after sugar and honey have dissolved to prevent burning and let candy hit the hard crack stage of 300°F. *(Candy is VERY particular. Do not overshoot this!!)*

3. Remove from heat and pour mixture onto a generously greased cookie sheet.

4. With a spatula, fold the honey candy over and over until it is cool enough to be able to be folded by hand. (It helps to have some latex gloves to prevent it from getting stuck to your hands.)

5. Fold and pull pieces of the cooled mixture off the larger slab with gloved hands. Pull pieces about 2" long and ½" thick, using kitchen shears to snip the pieces from the slab. Then hand roll them into tight, little spheres.

6. Set aside on a greased cookie sheet to harden for about 1 hour.

Shell Ingredients:
- ½ cup softened Unsalted Butter
- ¼ cup Sugar
- ¼ tsp Salt
- 1 large Egg White
- 1½ cup All-Purpose Flour

Cream Filling Ingredients:
- 2 tbsp Sugar
- 2 tbsp Flour
- 2 Egg Yolks
- ¼ cup Milk
- ½ cup Heavy Cream
- ½ tsp Vanilla Extract
- 2 tbsp Rum (optional)

Toppings:
- Grapes, Red and Green
- Blackberries
- Strawberries
- Orange
- Kiwi
- Whipped Cream

Glaze Ingredients:
- ½ cup Apricot Jam
- 2 tbsp Water

Shell Instructions:
1. Mix sugar, salt, egg white, and butter until smooth. Slowly add in flour and keep blending until smooth.
2. Press dough into 3 separate 6" tart pans. Make sure there's about a ¼" of dough covering each pan. Refrigerate dough for 30 minutes.
3. Preheat oven to 375°F. Bake tart shells for 12 minutes or until golden brown. Place on a wire rack to cool. Remove tart shells from pans when they are cool to touch.

Filling Instructions:
4. Beat egg yolks lightly. Add in milk and rum (optional), mix well.
5. In a saucepan, add flour and sugar, then pour in the milk mix. Raise heat to medium and bring to a boil. Stir constantly until thickened.
6. Set up an ice bath by placing a small bowl in a larger bowl that is partially filled with water and ice. Pour heavy cream into the small bowl and set aside.
5. Reheat milk mix over medium heat until just hot. *(Do not let it boil! If it does, the milk will curdle and separate into a mess and you can't fix that.)*

Assembly Instructions:
9. Use our recipe in the glossary to make some whipped cream, or use store-bought.
10. In the cooled tart shells, add in filling, then layer on whipped cream. Top with your fruit of choice.
11. Finish it off with the glaze. In a small saucepan, heat apricot jam and 2 tbsp of water over medium heat. Once thickened, remove from heat. Let cool and brush on top of fruit to make it shine.

Fruit Cake

Cake Ingredients:
- 4 large Eggs
- 1½ cup Sugar
- 1½ cup Flour
- 4 tbsp Unsalted Melted Butter
- 5 tbsp Milk

Simple Syrup Ingredients:
- 1 cup Sugar
- 1 cup Water

Frosting Ingredients:
- 2 cups Heavy Cream
- 4 tbsp Powdered Sugar

Toppings:
- Grapes, Red and Green
- Blackberries
- Strawberries
- Orange, sliced
- Kiwi, sliced

Cake Instructions:
1. Preheat oven to 350°F.
2. Whisk eggs in a bowl, add sugar and stir. Put the bowl of egg mixture over a pot of hot water and mix until sugar is dissolved and is warm to touch.
3. Beat the mixture on high for 3 to 4 minutes, then lower the speed and beat for 1 additional minute. (We are making a genoise cake. To make the cake rise, we beat air into the eggs rather than use chemical leavening agents like baking soda or baking powder.)
4. In small batches, add the flour to the batter and mix until incorporated.
5. Add melted butter and milk. Fold with spatula until blended. Pour into a 9" round cake pan and bake until golden, 30 to 35 minutes.
6. Slice off just enough of the top of cake to make it nice and level, then cut in half.

Simple Syrup Instructions:
7. Mix equal parts sugar and water in a pan over medium heat and stir until sugar is dissolved.
8. Remove from heat and let cool to room temperature.

Frosting Instructions:
9. Combine heavy cream and powdered sugar in a bowl and whip until soft peaks form.
10. Eat some while no one is looking.

Assembly Instructions:
11. Allow cake to cool completely before moving forward.
12. Coat the tops of your two cake halves with simple syrup.
13. Place one cake half on a serving plate and cover the top with frosting.
14. Place a thin layer of sliced strawberries on top of the frosting, followed by another layer of frosting.
15. Place the second half of cake on top and then frost the entire cake evenly.
16. Decorate the top of the frosted cake with whatever fruits you desire.
17. Slice and serve.

Nutcake

Ingredients:
- 1 cup Sugar
- ½ cup softened Unsalted Butter
- 2 large Eggs
- 1 tsp Vanilla Extract
- 2 cups All-Purpose Flour
- ½ tsp Baking Soda
- ½ tsp Baking Powder
- ½ tsp Salt
- 1 cup Chopped Walnuts
- ½ cup Pistachios, deshelled (garnish)

Instructions:
1. Preheat oven to 350°F.
2. In a large bowl, cream together sugar and butter.
3. Add eggs and vanilla. Beat until fluffy.
4. In another bowl, mix flour, baking soda, baking powder and salt. Add this to your other bowl a few spoonfuls at a time, while mixing together. Fold in walnuts.
5. Pour into a greased 9"x5" loaf pan. Bake for 45 to 50 minutes or until brown.
6. Cool in pan for 10 minutes then remove and transfer to cooling rack. Garnish with pistachios and serve with softened butter.

Ingredients:
- 2 cups White Sugar
- 1 cup Water
- ¾ cup Light Corn Syrup
- ¼ cup Pomegranate or Grape Juice
- Powdered Sugar
- Candy Thermometer
- Hammer

Instructions:

1. Prepare a 9"x9" pan by covering it in parchment paper and dusting it with powdered sugar. Set aside for now.

2. In a heavy 2-quart saucepan, combine the white sugar, water, and corn syrup. Cook over medium heat, stirring constantly, until the sugar is dissolved with the water and syrup.

3. Stir gently after sugar is dissolved to prevent burning. Heat candy to the hard crack stage, 300°F. *(Candy thermometer is a MUST for this recipe!!)*

4. Remove from heat and slowly add in the pomegranate or grape juice. Pour the hot candy into the prepared 9"x9" pan from earlier.

5. Let candy harden and cool completely, then break into chunks with a hammer. *(Stress release and candy, who could ask for more?)*

DIAMOND

AMBER

RUBY

SAPPHIRE

TOPAZ

OPAL

Tres Crepes

Ingredients:
-2 tbsp Melted Butter
-1½ cups Milk
-⅔ cup All-Purpose Flour
-½ tsp Salt
-3 large Eggs
-1 tsp Vanilla Extract

Toppings:
-Whipped Cream
-Honey
-Raspberries
-Butter
-Powdered Sugar
-Whatever You Want!

Instructions:
1. In a medium bowl, beat the melted butter, milk, eggs, salt, flour and vanilla until smooth. Cover and refrigerate for about 2 hours for bubbles to subside.
2. Brush bottom of a non-stick pan with butter over medium heat.
3. Pour ¼ cup of batter into the pan. If needed, spread with a metal spatula, and cook until the top sets and underside is lighted browned, about 2 minutes.
4. Jostle pan gently so crepe comes loose, then flip and cook the other side for 30 seconds.
5. Top your crepes with fresh whipped cream *(see our glossary for the recipe)* and raspberries, or keep it simple with a pad of butter. Honey and powdered sugar works great too!

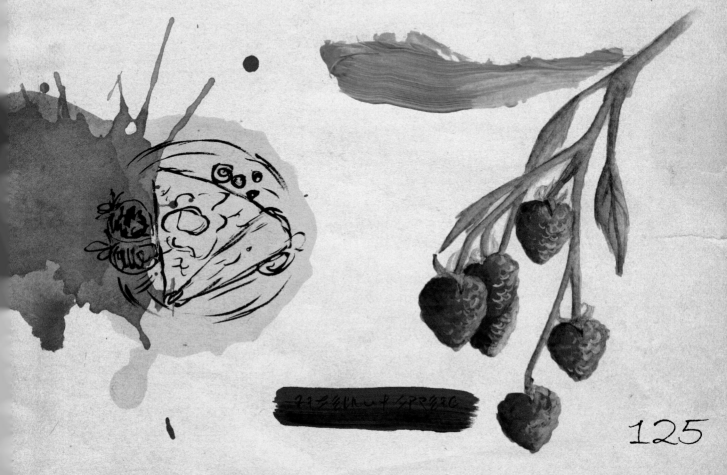

Wheat Bread

Ingredients:
- ⅓ cup Brown Sugar
- 1 tbsp Brown Sugar (extra)
- 2 cups Warm Water
- 1 cup Hot Water
- 2 packages Active Dry Yeast
- 5 cups Whole Wheat Flour
- ¾ cup Powdered Milk
- 2 tsp Salt
- ⅓ cup Vegetable Oil

Instructions:

1. In a small bowl, mix 2 cups of warm water with 2 packets of yeast. Add 1 tbsp of brown sugar to the mixture. Let everything dissolve and set aside.

2. In a stand mixer with a dough hook, add in 4 cups flour, powdered milk, ⅓ cup of brown sugar, and salt.

3. On low speed, beat the flour mixture for 15 seconds. Slowly add yeast mix and oil. Next add in the rest of the flour a little bit at a time until the dough starts to cling to the hook. Continue to mix the dough for two more minutes on low speed. *(Alternative instructions listed at the bottom of the page.)*

4. Remove dough from the mixer and place it in a greased bowl. Cover with plastic wrap and keep it in a warm place until it expands to about double the initial size. This should take about an hour.

5. Remove the dough from the bowl and place on a flour-covered surface. Punch the dough down to force out some of the air bubbles before dividing the dough in half.

6. Form both halves into loaves and place on a greased pan. Cover loosely with plastic wrap and let sit 45 to 60 minutes.

7. If you don't want to make two loaves right now, that's ok. Store one of the loaves in the fridge to bake in the next day or so. For now, preheat oven to 450°F.

8. Place a metal pan on the lowest rack of the oven.

9. Unwrap the dough you want to bake and make 2 to 3 deep ½" cuts on the top of the loaf. Place on a parchment paper lined baking sheet. Put your bread on the middle rack of the oven, above the other pan. Pour the hot water into the preheated pan to help steam your loaf.

10. Bake bread until golden brown, about 20-30 minutes.

11. Remove from oven. Immediately remove bread from the pan. Place on a cooling rack, eat while still warm.

Do you want to feel more like you're making this in the wild and/or don't own a stand mixer? No problem! Kneading by hand works just as well so long as you don't mind getting your hands messy:

1. In a large mixing bowl, combine the flour, powdered milk, ⅓ cup brown sugar, and salt by hand.

2. Create a well in the center of the bowl, and pour in your yeast mix from step 1 and the vegetable oil. Mix and combine by hand until you have a nice sticky dough ball, about 2½ minutes.

3. On a lightly floured surface, knead the dough aggressively. Push the dough outwards with the base of your palm, fold it back over on itself, give it a quarter turn and repeat. As dough becomes more resistant and less sticky, you may also lift the dough and smack it down on your surface to elongate and fold back on itself rather than pushing it. Knead as much as your arms are willing to give. *(To test gluten development, cut off a 1" piece of dough and stretch it out into a thin square. You can tell the dough is ready when it can be stretched thin with minimal breakage and is slightly translucent. This is a bit trickier with wheat flour, but works just the same.)*

Ice Cream Ingredients:
- 1 cup Whole Milk
- 2 cups Heavy Cream
- A pinch of Salt
- ¾ cup Sugar
- 1 Vanilla Bean
- 1 tsp Vanilla Extract
- 5 large Egg Yolks

Cone Ingredients:
- 2 large Egg Whites
- ¼ cup Brown Sugar
- 2 tbsp Whole Milk
- ¼ tsp Vanilla Extract
- 2 tbsp Butter, melted
- ½ cup All-Purpose Flour

Ice Cream Instructions:

1. Split the vanilla bean down the middle with a knife and set aside.

2. In a small saucepan, add the milk, sugar, and salt over medium heat. Stir until the sugar starts to dissolve.

3. Scrape the seeds from the vanilla bean into the milk mix, then add the bean pod. Once the sugar is completely dissolved, cover the pot and remove from heat. Let the mixture rest for 30 to 60 minutes to infuse the vanilla. Afterwards, remove the bean pod.

4. Set up an ice bath by placing a small bowl in a larger bowl that is partially filled with water and ice. Pour heavy cream into the small bowl and set aside.

5. Reheat milk mix over medium heat until just hot. *(Do not let it boil! If it does, the milk will curdle and separate into a mess and you can't fix that.)*

6. Seperate the egg yolks from the egg whites. Save 2 of the eggs whites for making the cones and use the other 3 egg whites for a breakfast omelet *(low in calories and fat-free)*. Whisk the yolks and gently pour about ¼ of the warm milk mix in.

7. Pour the yolk mix into the rest of the milk mix. Whisk quickly so no bands of yolk form. *(This is your custard.)*

8. Cook the custard over low heat, stirring constantly until it thickens enough to coat the back of a spatula. *(Egg proteins start to form a mesh that thickens the mixture. The temperature of the custard should be 175-180°F and should take 10 to 15 minutes.)*

9. Pour the custard through a strainer into the heavy cream in your ice bath. Add vanilla extract and stir until cool.

10. Once cool, cover the ice cream mixture with plastic wrap and put it in the freezer.

11. After 45 minutes, remove the ice cream from the freezer. Beat the ice cream to break up any frozen sections. Once broken up, add back to the freezer. *(The creamier the ice cream, the better!)*

12. Continue to check the ice cream every 30 minutes. Beat often to break up any forming ice crystals. It will likely take 3-4 hours to be ready. This will make a nice and airy ice cream. Keep in the freezer.

Cone Instructions:

13. Place the 2 egg whites saved from the ice cream into a small bowl.

14. In a small mixing bowl, add in brown sugar and egg whites. Mix until glossy.

15. Add milk, vanilla, melted butter, and flour. Whisk until smooth.

16. Make a cone shape out of aluminum foil. This will act as a template for your cone. *(Build it sturdy!)*

17. Put a parchment-lined baking pan in the oven and set it to preheat to 400° F.

18. Once at temperature, take out the baking pan and spread out the mix in a circle until it's around 6" in diameter and thin on the parchment.

19. Place in oven and bake for 8 minutes. *(You will have to move fast and also protect yourself from getting burned in this next step, so grab some pot holders and watch out!)*

20. Once ready, remove the pan from the oven and work fast by wrapping the cone around the aluminum foil template. The cone will harden super fast. *(If they get too stiff as you are trying to roll them onto the template, pop the whole thing back in the oven for a minute until soft.)*

21. Let your cone cool on the template. Once it is just slightly warm, scoop out a few dollops of your ice cream and enjoy a tasty ice cream cone! *(Wow, I can't believe I burned myself trying to make ice cream. That must be a glitch or something.)*

Monster Cake

Cake Ingredients:
- 2 cups Water
- 1 cup Unsweetened Dark Cocoa Powder
- 2¾ cups All-purpose Flour
- 2 tsp Baking Soda
- ½ tsp Baking Powder
- ½ tsp Salt
- 1 cup Unsalted Butter, softened
- 2¼ cups White Sugar
- 4 large Eggs
- 1½ tsp Vanilla Extract
- ½ cup White Chocolate Chips

Frosting Ingredients:
- ½ cup Blackberries
- 6 tbsp Unsalted Butter, softened
- 6 tbsp Cream Cheese, softened
- 2½ cups Powdered Sugar
- ½ tsp Vanilla Extract

Dark Cream Ingredients:
- 2 cups Heavy Cream
- ¼ cup Unsweetened Dark Cocoa Powder
- ½ cup Powdered Sugar

Horn Ingredients:
- 1 8oz Bar of Baking White Chocolate

Cake Instructions:
1. Preheat oven to 350°F. Grease three, 9" round cake pans.
2. Add water to a saucepan over medium-high heat. Remove when boiling.
2. In a medium bowl, pour boiling water over cocoa and whisk until smooth. Let mixture cool.
3. In a small bowl, sift together flour, baking soda, baking powder, and salt. Set aside.
4. In a large bowl, cream butter and sugar together until light and fluffy. Beat in eggs, one at a time, then stir in vanilla. Add in flour mixture, cocoa powder, and white chocolate chips. Stir well.
5. Spread batter evenly between the three prepared pans and bake for 25 to 30 minutes. Remove and set aside to cool.

Frosting Instructions:
6. Place fresh blackberries in a food processor and process until puréed. Place a fine mesh sieve over a small bowl and press the berry purée through the sieve. Discard the seeds. *(They'll just get stuck in your teeth or fangs.)*
7. Pour the berry purée into a small saucepan and cook over a low heat until thickened, about 5 to 7 minutes. Remove from heat and pour into another bowl to let cool completely.
8. In a large mixing bowl, beat butter and cream cheese with an electric mixer until smooth then add one cup of powdered sugar and beat until smooth.
9. Add vanilla, powdered sugar, and blackberry purée to taste. Make sure to taste test often to find the right balance of blackberry flavoring. Beat until light and fluffy

Dark Cream Instructions:
10. *This is a little variation on our standard whipped cream recipe from the glossary, so pay attention.* Place a metal mixing bowl and beaters in the freezer for 15 minutes.
11. Remove the bowl from the freezer. Add heavy cream, cocoa powder, and powdered sugar. Beat with an electric mixer until stiff peaks form, 4 to 5 minutes.

Horn Instructions:
12. Break up the white chocolate bar and microwave it for 30 seconds on high. If it isn't fully melted, microwave in 10-second intervals, stirring after each, until fully melted.
13. Add some leftover blackberry purée from the frosting stage to the melted chocolate and put in a piping bag. *(Feel free to use a piping tip with a piping bag if you happen to own a set. If you don't have a piping bag, you can cut off a bottom corner of a plastic bag. Don't cut off too much or it will make a huge hole.)*
14. Pipe the chocolate into little horn shapes on parchment paper. Place in the freezer until stiff, about 10 minutes.

Assembly Instructions:
15. Cut out 3" circles from cake pans. Stack on top of one another with a layer of filling between them. Dust the top of the cake with cocoa powder. Add the dark cream into a piping bag and create a chocolate swirl on the top of the cakes. Mount the horns in the cream.
16. Enjoy this dangerous dessert!

Monster Curry

Curry Ingredients:
- 4 tbsp Olive Oil
- ½ cup Onion, sliced
- 2 cloves Garlic, minced
- 1 cup Purple Potatoes, chunked (or Red Potatoes)
- ½ cup Purple Carrots, chunked (or Orange Carrots)
- 1 cup Red Cabbage, minced
- 1 lb Boneless Skinless Chicken Breasts, cubed
- 1 tbsp Tomato Paste
- 1 tbsp Ground Ginger
- 2 tbsp Garam Masala
- 2 tbsp Curry Powder
- 1 tsp Ground Turmeric
- ½ tbsp Ground Cayenne
- ½ tbsp Fenugreek Powder
- ½ tbsp Ground Coriander
- ½ tbsp Ground Cumin
- 2 cup Coconut Cream
- ½ tsp Salt
- ½ tsp Sugar

Monster Glaze Ingredients:
- ½ cup Purple Cabbage, sliced
- ½ cup Blackberries
- ½ Red Apple
- ¾ cup Sugar
- 2 tbsp Honey
- 2 tsp Cornstarch
- 2 tbsp Lemon Juice

Black Rice Ingredients:
- 1 cup Black Rice (or Jasmine Rice)
- 6 cups Water
- A generous pinch of Salt

Curry Instructions:
1. In a saucepan over medium heat, add oil. Once hot, add onion, carrot, and garlic. Cook until onions are translucent and garlic is fragrant, about 5 minutes.
2. Add ginger, garam masala, curry powder, turmeric, cayenne, fenugreek powder, coriander, cumin, sugar, and salt to vegetables. Add a bit of water if you want to thin it out, it's up to you how thick you want your curry.
3. Add chunked potatoes and cook until they are fork tender, about 10 to 15 minutes.
4. Cut chicken into rough cubes and add to the mix. Cover and let simmer until cooked all the way through, 8 to 10 minutes.
5. Mix in tomato paste, minced cabbage, and coconut cream. Let the mix simmer until everything is cooked and thickened.

Monster Glaze Instructions:
6. In a saucepan over low heat, add berries and stir. Once juice starts to leak from berries, mash them with a fork or spoon. Remove from heat.
7. Press the blackberry goo one spoonful at a time through a fine-mesh sieve to remove seeds. Discard seeds. Pour seedless goo into a blender and let cool.
8. Add 3 tablespoons of cold water to cornstarch and gently mix into a slurry.
9. Pour cornstarch mixture into the blender with the blackberry goo along with remaining ingredients.
10. Blend until smooth and evil.

Black Rice Instructions:
11. In a large pot, add water and a large pinch of salt and heat over medium high. Bring to a boil and add rice.
12. Let simmer uncovered until tender, about 20 to 25 minutes. Drain and fluff with a fork.

Assembly Instructions:
13. Plate yourself a healthy serving of rice. Spoon curry over the rice and add some glaze to the plate.
14. With each bite, try mixing a little bit of curry, rice and glaze. The sweet and spicy combo is monstrously good! The amount of carbs, on the other hand, is pure evil.

Monster Rice Balls

Ingredients:
- 1 cup Short Grain White Rice
- 1 Tbsp Wild Rice (optional)
- ½ cup Water
- 1 Red Onion, finely diced
- ¼ cup Distilled White Vinegar
- ¼ cup Apple Cider Vinegar
- 1½ tbsp Honey
- 1½ tsp Sea Salt
- ¼ tsp Red Pepper Flakes
- 4 small Cucumbers, finely diced
- A pinch Pink Sea Salt
- Nori

Instructions:

1. ***Prepare the rice according to the recipe in our glossary.*** Use both short grain and wild rice if you have both. If not, stick with short grain only. It'll still be good!

2. In a small saucepan over medium high heat, combine vinegars, honey, salt, pepper flakes and half a cup of water. Bring to a gentle simmer.

3. Pour vinegar mixture into a jar and add red onions and cucumber. Let cool to room temperature and marinate for 1 to 3 hours, or even overnight, before serving.

4. Dip your hands in water and rub salt on them to prevent the rice from sticking to your hands. ***(Wash your hands first!)***

5. Plate the rice by forming it into a pyramid shape. Poke a hole in the center with your finger. Add a spoonful of cucumber and onion mix inside the hole and seal it up with more rice. Form into a rice ball shape.

6. Use a piece of nori to hold each sticky riceball and sprinkle them with a pinch of pink sea salt

7. Consume. **CONSUME.**

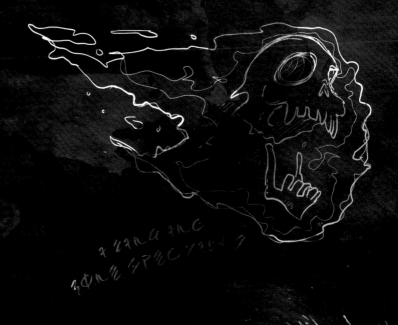

Monster Soup

Ingredients:
- 1 lb Purple Potatoes, diced (or Red Potatoes)
- 2 tbsp Butter
- 6 strips Bacon, diced
- 6 Purple Carrots, peeled and diced (or Orange Carrots)
- 2 cups Milk, warmed
- 1 cup Yellow Onion, finely diced
- 3 cloves Garlic, minced
- 1 tsp Dried Oregano
- ¾ tsp Ground Ginger
- ½ tsp Ground Cumin
- ½ tsp Salt
- ½ tsp Black Pepper
- 3 cups Vegetable Broth
- ¼ cup All-Purpose Flour
- Heavy Cream (garnish)

Instructions:
1. In a large pot over medium high heat, add butter and diced bacon, cook until crispy. Remove bacon from the pot and leave about 2 to 3 tablespoons of bacon drippings inside the pot.
2. Add in the onions and sauté for 5 minutes.
3. Next, add in the garlic and sauté till fragrant, about 2 minutes. Sprinkle flour over the onions and add in diced potatoes, vegetable broth, milk, salt, pepper, oregano, ginger, cumin, and carrots.
4. Bring to a boil and cook until potatoes are tender, about 10 minutes. Reduce heat to simmer and ladle ⅓ of the soup into a blender. Purée until smooth. Return the purée to the rest of the soup.
5. Add the bacon back in, stir well and simmer soup for 15 minutes.
6. Ladle into a bowl and decorate with esoteric and occult symbols using heavy cream. Oh, and salt and pepper to taste. *(Be careful not to summon an Eldritch Horror when decorating soup, they don't taste very good unless you turn them into calamari.)*

Rock Spice Ingredients:
- 2 tbsp Onion Powder
- 2 tbsp Garlic Powder
- 2 tbsp Dried Oregano
- 2 tbsp Dried Basil
- 1 tbsp Dried Thyme
- 1 tbsp Black Pepper
- 1 tbsp Ground White Pepper
- 1 tbsp Ground Cayenne
- 5 tbsp Paprika
- 3 tbsp Salt

Stew Ingredients:
- 3 cups Low Sodium Vegetable Stock
- 1 Yellow Onion, diced
- 1 cup All-Purpose Flour
- 3 cloves Garlic, minced
- 1 tbsp Vegetable Oil
- 1 cup Dry Red Wine
- 3 Purple Sweet Potatoes, diced (or Yams)
- 6 oz Tomato Sauce
- 1 tbsp Dried Italian Herbs
- 1 lb Deveined Shrimp
- 1 lb Beef Chuck Stew Meat
- 6 strips Bacon, diced
- 1 cup of Black Rice (or Jasmine Rice)
- 12 oz. Andouille Sausage, sliced
- 2 Purple Carrots, diced (or Orange Carrots)
- 2 sprigs Thyme
- ½ tsp Hot Sauce
- 2 tbsp Worcestershire Sauce
- 2 tsp Rock Spice
- ½ lb Okra, thinly sliced
- 1 tbsp Butter

Monster Stew

Instructions:

1. Make your Rock Spice by mixing all the ingredients in a small bowl. Mix until combined. You can even put it in a spice blender to improve the texture. *(Feel free to use leftover Rock Spice on any meat recipes you've made.)*

2. In a large pot over medium high heat, add diced bacon and cook until crispy.

3. Remove bacon from the pot and leave in all the bacon drippings. Add flour and wisk together over medium low heat to form a smooth roux. It is ok, you can nibble on some bacon while you cook.

4. Add the purple potatoes, garlic, onion, carrots, and sausage. Mix with the roux over medium low heat and cook until vegetables are tender, 10 to 15 minutes. Remove from heat.

5. In a large Dutch oven, add oil and brown the beef on all sides over medium high heat. Add in the tomato sauce, dried Italian herbs and mix well.

6. Next, add the stock, wine and roux mix. Let it come to a boil, then reduce heat to a simmer and leave covered for 1 hour.

7. Add the rice then cover again. Let simmer for another 15 minutes. *(If the stew looks like it needs more stock, add an extra cup.)*

8. In a pan with 1 tbsp butter, cook the thinly sliced okra over medium heat for 15 minutes. Remove okra and add it to the stew with the bacon, shrimp, Rock Spice, thyme, hot sauce and Worcestershire Sauce.

9. Gently stir together then cover. Let simmer for 20 to 30 minutes then enjoy your sinfully savory stew.

This drink contains alcohol. Only make this if you are 21 years of age or older and partake at your own risk!

Noble Pursuit

Ingredients:
- 1½ cup Watermelon Chunks
- 1 cup Dragon Fruit Chunks
- 2 tbsp Lime Juice
- 2½ oz Tequila
- 2 tsp Triple Sec
(or ¼ cup Sparkling Water
for non alcoholic)
- 10 Ice Cubes
- 1 small Lime (garnish)
- 2 tbsp Pink Sea Salt (or Sea Salt)
- 2 tbsp Sugar

Instructions:
1. Cut open a watermelon and a dragon fruit and dice both into chunks. Set aside a few pieces of watermelon for garnish. Place 1½ cups of the watermelon and 1 cup of the dragon fruit on a baking sheet. Place baking sheet in the freezer until the fruit is frozen solid completely.

2. In a blender, combine fruit, lime juice, tequila, triple sec (or sparkling water), and ice cubes. Blend until smooth.

3. On a small plate, combine salt and sugar. Drizzle lime juice on the rim of the glass and dip into the salt-sugar mix to coat the rim. Pour in the blended drink and garnish with unfrozen watermelon. Wow, this legendary drink is ready to aid you on your quest to have a good time!

Electro Elixir

Ingredients:
- 1 Dragon Fruit
- 8 leaves Mint
- 1 tsp Sugar
- 1 oz Lime Juice
- 2 oz White Rum
- 2 oz Club Soda
- 3 oz Pineapple Juice
- 1 small Lime
- Ice Cubes

Instructions:
1. Cut lime into wedges, dice about a quarter of a dragon fruit into cubes, and crush up mint leaves. Drop them all into the bottom of a flat-bottomed glass.
2. Add sugar, and muddle with mint, lime, and dragon fruit.
3. Pour in lime juice and muddle again.
4. Top with ice cubes, white rum, pineapple juice, and club soda. Give the entire thing a nice stir and this drink is done! Cheers! (*Don't drink and run in a thunderstorm.*)

Spicy Elixir

Ingredients:
- Mango Nectar
- 2 oz Tequila (or Pineapple Juice)
- 1 oz Lime Juice
- 1 fresh Red Hot Cherry Pepper
- 1 small Lime (garnish)
- Salt
- 1 tbsp Chili Powder
- Ice Cubes

Instructions:
1. On a small plate, combine salt and chili powder. Drizzle lime juice on the rim of a small glass. Dip the glass into the salt-chili powder mix to coat the rim.
2. Use a garlic press to juice a fresh cherry pepper. Squeeze the juice into the coated glass. Be careful handling the cherry pepper juice and make sure they don't get in your eyes. Wash your hands thoroughly after handling them.
3. Pour the lime juice and tequila (or pineapple juice) into the glass and add a few ice cubes. Top off the glass with mango nectar.
4. Garnish with a slice of lime or a little pepper! Watch out, this drink is sweet, salty, and hot! (*I like to enjoy this drink with a few hot sauce-covered mango slices, a handful of rambutans, and some lime.*)

145

Sneaky Elixir

Ingredients:
-2 oz fresh Blueberries
-2 oz fresh Blackberries
-2 oz Tequila
-1 cup Water
-1 cup Sugar
-1 small Lemon
-Club Soda
- Ice Cubes

Instructions:

1. In a small saucepan over medium high heat, add one cup of water and one cup of sugar. Stir until sugar dissolves. This is a basic simple syrup.

2. Once the simple syrup starts to boil, slice the lemon into wedges, squeeze the juice into the syrup, and drop the wedges in to the pan. Cover and remove from heat. Let it sit for one hour to infuse with lemon.

3. In a cocktail shaker, add berries, 1 oz of your lemon simple syrup, and tequila. Muddle the berries with the handle of a wooden spoon until the mixture is mostly liquid.

4. Place ice in the shaker and shake until frost forms on the outside of the shaker.

5. Pour mixture into a chilled glass and top with as much club soda as you'd like. Garnish with lemon rind. The sneaky elixir is done! *(If made perfectly you'll gain +3 sneak, or is that just the booze talking? No wait, it is totally the tequila. I am not fooling anyone.)*

Fairy Tonic

Ingredients:
- 1 oz White Rum
- ½ oz Lemon Juice
- 2 oz Cranberry Mango Juice
- ⅛ tsp Pearl Dust Edible Glitter
- Tonic
- Strawberries (garnish)
- Ice Cubes

Instructions:

1. Pour the rum and juices into a chilled, tall glass.

2. Gently add the pearl dust. Stir and watch the magic.

3. Add a few ice cubes and top off the glass with as much tonic as you'd like.

4. Garnish with some thinly sliced strawberries. They almost look like fairy wings.

149

Ingredients:
- 1 lb 90/10 Lean Ground Beef
- 1 lb Ground Pork
- ½ cup Italian Seasoned Breadcrumbs
- ½ cup Panko Breadcrumbs
- 1 tbsp Dried Italian Seasoning
- ¼ cup Grated Parmesan Cheese
- 2 tbsp Whole Milk
- 1 large Egg
- 2 sprigs Basil, finely chopped
- 2 Onions, finely chopped
- 2 Red Bell Peppers, finely chopped
- 2 cloves Garlic, finely chopped
- Extra Virgin Olive Oil
- 1 tsp Smoked Paprika
- ½ tsp Ground Cayenne
- 1 tsp Sugar
- 1 tsp Ground Cumin
- 14 oz can Crushed Tomatoes
- Salt and Black Pepper
- 4 Large Eggs
- 1 tsp Ground Coriander
- 1 tsp Chives
- 1 Lime

Instructions:
1. In a large bowl, add both meats, milk, egg, breadcrumbs, cheese, italian seasoning and basil. Mix until everything is well incorporated.
2. Form meat mixture into meatballs that are just a little smaller than your palm. *(Unless you're a giant. Then make them very small compared to your giant hands.)*
3. In a cast-iron skillet on medium heat, add about a ¼" of oil. Fry the meatballs until they are browned on all sides and cooked through, about 15 minutes.
4. Remove meat from skillet and use the leftover oil to fry onions, red pepper, and garlic until golden brown and tender, 3 to 4 minutes.
5. Add all the dry spices, tomatoes, and sugar. Mix well and let simmer on low for 5 to 10 minutes. Season with salt and pepper to taste.
6. Put the meatballs back in the pan and coat with the tomato base.
7. Use a wooden spoon to make 4 depressions in the sauce. Crack an egg into each hole. Cover and cook until egg whites are set, 5 to 10 minutes.
8. Sprinkle coriander, chives, and squeeze lime juice to taste. Eat it right out of the skillet. *(Be careful where you set the hot skillet, though! Use a trivet!)*

Cuccos and Waffles

Waffle Ingredients:
-2 large Eggs
-1¾ cups Buttermilk
-1 stick Unsalted Butter
-1¾ cups All-Purpose Flour
-2 tbsp Light Brown Sugar
-2 tbsp Baking Powder
-1 tsp Baking Soda
-1 tsp Salt

Waffle Instructions:
1. In a bowl, whisk together dry ingredients.
2. Melt butter and let cool until it's at room temperature.
3. In another bowl, whisk eggs, buttermilk, and melted butter until homogenous.
4. Add dry ingredients and whisk until smooth.
5. Heat waffle iron and grease lightly with butter so your waffles don't stick. Ladle batter onto the iron, close, and cook until golden brown.
6. Set waffles aside and wrap in aluminum foil to keep warm.

Sunbutter Syrup Ingredients:
-¼ cup Sunbutter
-¼ cup Maple Syrup

Sunbutter Syrup Instructions:
7. Mix sunbutter and maple syrup until homogeneous.
8. *What? Did you expect every recipe to be difficult? Sometimes, the simplest stuff in life is also the best. Like Sunbutter Syrup.*

Fried Chicken Ingredients:
-8 Chicken Wings/Drumsticks
-2 cups Buttermilk
-2 tbsp Hot Sauce
-2 tbsp Worcestershire Sauce
-2½ cups All-Purpose Flour
-4 tbsp Cornstarch
-3 tbsp Seasoned Salt
-2 tbsp Paprika
-2 tbsp Black Pepper
-1 tsp Garlic Salt
-1 tbsp Onion Powder
-Frying Oil

Fried Chicken Instructions:
9. In a medium-sized bowl, whisk together buttermilk, hot sauce, and worcestershire sauce. Add chicken into a zippered plastic bag and pour in the marinade mix. Seal bag and marinate in the refrigerator for at least 2 hours or up to 8 hours. *(Don't leave it overnight! The chicken will start to break down due to acids in the marinade. There's no real flavor benefit to leaving it over 8 hours anyway.)*
10. In a bowl, combine flour, cornstarch, garlic salt, onion powder, seasoned salt, paprika, and black pepper.
11. Dredge the chicken in the flour mix. Coat well.
12. Over medium high heat, add a little under 1" of frying oil to a cast-iron skillet. *(Don't use olive oil, it has a low smoke point. The smoke point is the temperature at which an oil's fats begin to break down and burn, hence the smoke. It will leave your chicken with a gross, scorched flavor.)*
13. Check to see if your oil is hot. *(I have a trick to test this. Toss a tiny bit of flour in the oil and see if it begins to fry and sizzle. If it does, the oil is ready.)*
14. Add chicken to the pan, 3 or 4 at a time to prevent crowding. Fry for 6-8 minutes, turning occasionally with tongs, until the chicken is crispy and a deep golden brown.
15. Remove chicken from pan and place on paper towels to wick away excess oil.
16. To serve, place your waffles on a plate and top with butter. Place the chicken on top of the waffles and drizzle sunbutter syrup over the whole thing.

153

Chu Jelly

Ingredients:
- 3 cups Water
- 3 tbsp dried Butterfly Pea Flowers
- 2 tbsp Honey
- 1 packet Unflavored Gelatin
- 1 cup Warm Water
- 1 cup Cold Water

Instructions:

1. Steep some tea by filling a hot pan with 3 cups of water and the dried Butterfly Pea Flowers. Once the tea turns a brilliant dark blue, strain it into another pot.

2. Add honey, stir, and let dissolve.

3. Bloom a package of plain gelatin. This is done by adding it to a cup of warm water and breaking it up with a wooden spoon. Once the gelatin has dissolved, add it to the tea and stir until incorporated.

4. Add a cup of cold water.

5. Pour the tea gelatin mix into small, 1" dome-shaped moulds and refrigerate until firm; at least an hour but preferably overnight.

6. Run the bottoms of the moulds under hot water when you are ready to remove the jellies. They have a subtle, earthy flavor. Enjoy them with a side of tea or maybe on a cracker!

Monster Eyeballs

Iris Ingredients:
- ½ cup Cold Water
- ¼ cup Corn Syrup
- 2 packets Unflavored Gelatin
- ¼ cup Pineapple Juice
- Blackberries

Sclera Ingredients:
- ½ cup Cold Water
- ¼ cup Corn Syrup
- 2 packets Unflavored Gelatin
- ¼ cup Pomegranate Juice
- ¼ tsp Citric Acid Powder

Instructions:

1. In a medium pot, mix the cold water and corn syrup together. Slowly stir in the 2 packages of unflavored gelatin.

2. Raise heat to medium low, stirring constantly until smooth and fully dissolved, 5 to 10 minutes.

3. Add pineapple juice and mix well.

4. Skim the top of the mix to remove any film. *(This will ensure you have a nice, clear jelly!)*

(Fun fact: The little dark purple balls that comprise a blackberry are called drupelets. This will help the next step make sense)

5. Prepare a cake pop tray. Pick the blackberries apart and add about two blackberries' worth of drupelets to half of the mold, then fill halfway with the pineapple mix. These will be your irises.

6. Place the tray in the fridge to cool for about an hour.

7. Repeat steps 1-4 with pomegranate juice and citric acid powder instead of pineapple juice.

8. Once step 6 has been completed, fill in the mold with the irises the rest of the way with pomegranate mix.
Then fill the remaining empty mold. These will be your scleras.

9. Return the tray to the fridge and cool until firm.

10. Remove the scleras and irises from each mold. Stick the smooth bottom of each sclera to the corresponding smooth bottom of each iris to make complete eyeballs! *(You can gently wet the flat sides of each half with water to get them to stick better!)*

11. Store in the fridge until you're ready to eat some gummy eyes! Which can be as soon as you make them.

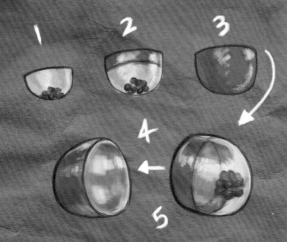

(Hey! Listen! This recipe is deceptively intricate so try picturing it in your head first! When I made it, I put sticky notes on the different mixtures so I didn't get mixed up.)

Sweet Potato Latte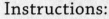

Ingredients:
- ½ Sweet Potato
- 1 tsp Ground Cinnamon
- 2 tbsp Honey
- 1 cup Whole Milk
- Whipped Cream (garnish)
- Almond Slices (garnish)

Instructions:

1. Poke several holes all over your sweet potato half with a fork.

2. Microwave until the sweet potato is fork-tender, about 4 minutes. If your potato is still hard, continue microwaving in 30-second intervals until you are able to stick a fork in it with no resistance. *(Depending on potato size and microwave, cooking time may vary.)*

3. Carefully peel the skin off your potato *(Don't burn yourself!)* and chop into medium sized chunks. Add to a blender with honey and cinnamon and set aside. *(Don't blend yet!)*

4. Heat milk in a pan over medium high heat until just steaming, then add to the blender. Blend until smooth.

5. Add the mix back to your pan and heat to your desired serving temperature. Pour into mugs and top with whipped cream *(recipe from our glossary)*, a sprinkle of cinnamon, and almond slices.

Cinnamon

Secret Medicine

Ingredients:
- 4 Strawberries
- 1 oz Grenadine
- 2 oz Tequila
- 1 oz Lime Juice
- Ice
- Ginger Ale

Instructions:
1. Wash and remove stems from the strawberries.
2. Drop the strawberries in an eight-ounce glass and lightly mash them with a muddler or wooden spoon handle.
3. Add the grenadine, tequila, and lime juice to the glass of strawberries.
4. Add several ice cubes to the glass, then top off with chilled ginger ale.

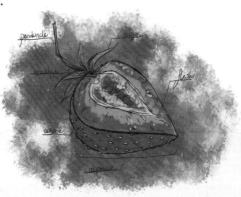

You ever notice how strawberries don't look quite like any other berry? Technically, they aren't berries at all! Strawberries are an 'aggregate fruit', a fusion of various parts of the plant. The little black dots you might mistake for seeds are actually called 'achene' and do in fact contain an even smaller seed inside. Strawberries are great on their own or with a myriad of other foodstuffs. You can eat them fresh, frozen, in a salad or a milkshake, spaghetti, or even a late night daiquiri. Wait, spaghetti!? Yep, strawberry spaghetti is a thing. Replace the meatballs in your red sauce with big, juicy strawberries for a unique twist on a classic dish.

161

Power Croissant

Ingredients:
- 2 tbsp Sugar
- 1½ tsp Salt
- 2 packages Active Dry Yeast
- 3 cups All-Purpose Flour
- 1¼ cup Milk
- 1 cup Unsalted Butter, cold
- 2 tbsp Unsalted Butter, melted
- 1 large Egg
- ¼ cup Powdered Sugar

Instructions:

1. In a large bowl, combine the sugar, salt, yeast, and 1 cup of flour. Set aside.
2. In a saucepan, warm the milk over low heat until the temperature hits 120-130°F.
3. On low speed, beat the warm milk into the dry mixture for 1 minute. Increase the speed to medium and slowly add in ½ cup of flour, scraping the sides of the bowl. Beat for 2 minutes.
4. Stir in 1 cup of flour and the melted butter. Beat for one more minute to make the dough soft.
5. Cover a smooth surface with the rest of the flour and place your dough on the surface. Knead the dough until it's smooth and elastic, about 10 minutes.
6. Cover your dough in plastic wrap and chill for 1 hour in the fridge.
7. Flatten cold butter into a thin rectangle, about ¼" thick, between two pieces of wax paper. Return butter to the fridge to retain shape. *(Don't let it get too warm, or else it will melt! You want the butter to stay chilled and keep its shape.)*

(Now for the hard part. Croissants are very difficult to get right. You have to 'laminate' the dough by folding the dough over itself with a thin layer of butter in between. You just have to do this a bunch.)

8. On a lightly floured surface, roll the dough into a long rectangle and place your butter rectangle right in the center. Fold the dough over the top of the butter.
9. Fold your dough into thirds and roll it out again. Turn your dough 90 degrees and fold it in thirds again, then roll it out again! Repeat this at least 5 times.

(If your butter starts to melt, return the whole thing to the fridge until it is stiff again. You want to continue this folding process until there's nice, smooth streaks of butter in your dough. This will yield that incredible flaky bread!)

10. Once you are happy with your streaks, wrap tightly with plastic wrap and chill for 1 more hour.

(Now for the fun part, making that crescent shape!)

11. Cut dough in half and return half to the fridge. *(You probably can't form all the dough before it starts to rise, but don't worry! You'll be back for it soon enough.)*
12. Roll out dough into a long rectangle with thickness of about ⅛", should be around 1' by 2'.
13. Use a pizza cutter or sharp knife to cut the dough into long, skinny triangles, about 6" at the hypotenuse. *(Remember back to grade school? That's the longest side of a triangle.)*
14. Take each triangle and roll starting with the wide end and rolling towards the pointed end.
15. Curve the two ends together to get that signature shape. *(I even press the dough together at the ends and sort of lock them into place. Huh, it kind of looks like a bracelet.)*

16. Place your crescents on a parchment lined baking sheet. Cover loosely with plastic wrap and allow to rise for 2 hours. *(Once you reach this step, you can return to the fridge for the other half of the dough you left behind.)*
17. Preheat the oven to 375°F.
18. Create an egg wash by whisking 1 egg in a small bowl. Gently brush onto the croissants.
19. Bake for 10 to 15 minutes or until golden brown and flaky.
20. Remove from the oven and set on a cooling rack for 20 minutes.
21. Sprinkle each croissant with powdered sugar
22. Enjoy your powerful breakfast to strengthen your day!

Volcano Cake

Ingredients:
- 8 oz Semi-Sweet Chocolate, finely chopped
- 2 cups Flour
- 1½ cups Sugar
- 1¼ cup Buttermilk
- ½ cups Shortening
- 3 large Eggs
- 1½ tsp Baking Soda
- 1 tsp Salt
- 1 tsp Vanilla Extract
- ½ tsp Double-Acting Baking Powder
- 1 cup Heavy Whipping Cream
- 4 oz Unsweetened Chocolate
- 1 White Chocolate Truffle
- Mixed Berry Jam

Instructions:

1. Preheat oven to 350°F.
2. Melt unsweetened chocolate over a double boiler.
3. In a large bowl, add the flour, sugar, buttermilk, shortening, eggs, melted chocolate, baking soda, salt, vanilla extract, and baking powder. Beat on low speed until well mixed, scraping the sides of the bowl as you go. Increase speed to high and beat for 5 minutes.
4. Pour batter into 2 greased, 9" cake pans. Bake for 25 to 30 minutes. (*Use a toothpick to check. If you insert a toothpick into the center of the cake and it comes out clean, the cake is ready!*)
5. Remove cakes from the pans and cool on a wire rack for 10 minutes.
6. Heat heavy whipping cream in a small saucepan over medium heat until it begins to gently simmer. Remove from heat.
7. In a mixing bowl, add the semi-sweet chocolate and pour the hot cream over it. Let it sit for 2 to 3 minutes, then slowly stir with a rubber spatula until fully combined into a ganache. Set aside.

(*This next step involves a lot of engineering, we are trying to make a 4 tier cake. You don't have to do this, you can just stack the two 9" cakes from the pans with a layer of ganache in between and add some frosting. But, if you're feeling adventurous, you can try this.*)

8. Use a 6" 4", 3", and 1" round cookie cutter to cut out the tiers of your cake from the cakes in the pans. (*I suggest cutting out the 6" and 1" section out of one cake pan while cutting the 4" and 3" out of the other.*)
9. Stack your cake cutouts on top of each other. Largest on the bottom, smallest on the top. Coat the bottom of each tier with mixed berry jam to help cement them in place. (***Try to get the order right, this isn't pineapple upside down cake.***)
10. Drizzle chocolate ganache over the top of the stacked cake and top with a white chocolate truffle. (*You can go a little overboard with decorating your beautiful creation. Make it look like it came right out of a dream!*)

Not sure what a double boiler is? Have no fear, for we have done the research for you. First you'll need two sauce pans of roughly the same size. Fill one pan with 1" to 2" of water and place over medium heat. Place the second pan on top of the first and add whatever ingredients you'd like to melt. Make sure the top pan does not touch the water. If you don't have a second pan you can use a metal bowl. Just make sure the bottom of the bowl does not touch the water. If this step is a bit too much, you can always do a quick and dirty melt using a microwave, or by placing the chocolate in a zippered bag and submerging it in a bowl of hot water. Double up on the bags so water doesn't get in! Introducing water creates 'seized chocolate', changing the texture to grainy and stiff. Basically the opposite of melted.

Bait

Ingredients:
- 1 lb lean 90/10 Ground Beef
- 1 lb Ground Pork
- ½ cup Italian Seasoned Breadcrumbs
- ½ cup Panko Breadcrumbs
- 1 tbsp dried Italian Seasoning
- ¼ cup grated Parmesan Cheese
- 2 tbsp Whole Milk
- 1 large Egg
- ¼ tbsp Red Pepper Flakes
- 1 tbsp Onion Powder
- ½ tbsp Garlic Salt
- 1 tsp dried Parsley
- ¼ cup Tomato Sauce
- 4 large Onions
- 16 oz Mozzarella Cheese (Block)
- 15 slices Bacon
- 4 stalks Bok Choy
- Toothpicks

Instructions:

1. Preheat oven to 425°F.

2. In a large bowl, combine beef, pork, both breadcrumbs, Italian seasoning, parmesan cheese, whole milk, egg, red pepper flakes, onion powder, garlic salt, tomato sauce, and parsley. Mix gently until the meat is well incorporated. *(Make sure you don't overmix the meat!)*

3. Chop off the ends of an onion and slit lengthwise to the center of the onion *(see illustration below)*. Peel off your first layer and discard it. Peel the rest of the layers off the onion so you end up with hollow shells. *(You can get more than one shell out of a single onion. If the shell snaps in two, don't worry! When we wrap it with bacon it will stay in place.)* Repeat until you have around 10 hollow shells.

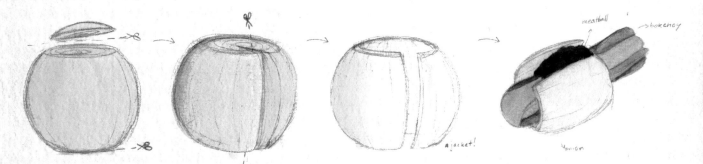

4. Dice the mozzarella cheese into small blocks. Cut the bok choy stalks into long pieces.

5. Place a piece of mozzarella cheese in the middle of a stalk of bok choy. Wrap it with a handful of meat mix to hold the cheese in place.

6. Slide each onion shell down the bok choy stalk so that it captures the meat ball in the middle of the stalk, tightly packing the meat within the shell.

7. Use 3 slices of bacon to wrap the onion shells. *(I suggest wrapping the first piece vertical and the other two pieces around the first, like an 'X.')* Hold the bacon in place with toothpicks jammed into the onion shell.

8. Place the bacon-wrapped onion meatballs on a wire rack on top of a pan so the grease can drip down. Bake for 40 minutes.

9. After that, take your hot fresh bites out of the oven! *(Well, don't take a hot fresh bite right away or you'll burn yourself. Learned that one the hard way.)*

10. Enjoy hot, but not too hot - makes a great bait. Dig in!

Water of Life

Ingredients:
- ½ cup Pomegranate Juice
- 1 Lime
- 2 cups Coconut Water
- 2 tbsp Raw Honey (or Maple Syrup)
- ⅛ tsp Himalayan Pink Salt

Instructions:
1. Cut the lime in half and juice both halves. *(Roll the lime around on a counter or smooth surface with some pressure before cutting to make the juicing easier!)*
2. Pour the lime juice and remaining ingredients into a blender. Blend until smooth.
3. Pour over ice or serve chilled.

Yeti Supreme Soup

Ingredients:
- 2 lbs edible Pumpkin (or Canned Pumpkin)
- 4 tbsp Olive Oil
- 4 cloves Garlic, minced
- ½ cup White Onion, chopped
- 4 cups Fish Stock (or Chicken Stock)
- 8 oz Goat Cheese
- 1½ cups Heavy Cream
- 1 cup Carrots, peeled and chunked
- 2 Potatoes, chunked
- 1 cup Celery, chopped
- 2 lbs Salmon Filet
- Salt and Black Pepper

Instructions:
1. Preheat oven to 350°F.
2. Make sure you have an edible pumpkin. Take your pumpkin, cut the top off, remove the guts and seeds, and cut into pieces. Bake in the oven for 15 minutes. Once the pumpkin is baked and softened, peel skin and cut into bite-sized chunks. *(You can also just use canned pumpkin (not pie mix) and skip the baking if edible varieties are out of season.)*
3. While your pumpkin is baking, cut onions and mince garlic.
4. Set aside a third of your garlic. Add the other two-thirds and the onions into a large pot with 2 tbsp of olive oil. Cook until browned on medium high heat.
5. Add in pumpkin and fish stock. Cover and cook at a simmer for 45 minutes.

6. Remove from heat, pour into a blender and purée. As you blend, add in your goat cheese and heavy cream.
7. In a large pot on medium high heat, add 2 tbsp of olive oil and the rest of your garlic. Cook until browned.
8. Add carrots, potatoes, and celery. Sauté for about 10 minutes.
9. Add the purée and cook on low heat for 10 to 15 minutes.
10. With a knife, score your salmon filet in 1" increments. Add salt and pepper to taste inside the cuts.
11. In a pan on medium high heat, add the salmon and cook skin side down first for 4 to 5 minutes. Flip to the other side, and cook for 3 more minutes. Finally, flip back so that the skin side is down. Take off heat and let it rest for 3 minutes. Cut your salmon into bite-sized pieces and add it to the soup.
12. Let simmer for 5 minutes before indulging in a big, warm bowl of it.
I heard it is very nutritious and will help with any cold!

Pumpkin Soup

Ingredients:
-2 lbs edible Pumpkin,
(or Canned Pumpkin)
-2 tbsp Butter
-1 large Onion, chopped
-3 cloves Garlic, minced
-1 large Apple, peeled,
cored and chopped
-½ tbsp Ground Ginger
-1 tsp Curry Powder
-1 tsp Ground Cayenne
-½ cup Celery, chopped
-4 large Carrots, peeled and chopped
-3 cups Vegetable Broth
-14 oz can Unsweetened Coconut Milk
-1 Bay Leaf
-Salt and Black Pepper

Instructions:
1. Preheat the oven to 350°F.
2. Make sure you have an edible pumpkin. *(The kind of pumpkins you buy for Halloween are edible but not as good as the varieties bred specifically for eating.)* Take your pumpkin, cut the top off, remove the guts and seeds, and cut into pieces. Bake in the oven for 15 minutes. Once the pumpkin is baked and softened, peel skin and cut into bite-sized chunks. *(You can also just use canned pumpkin (not pie mix) and skip the baking if edible varieties are out of season.)*
3. Add butter to a medium sauté pan on medium low heat. Once the butter has melted, add the onions, garlic, apple, ginger, curry powder, cayenne, celery, and carrots. Cook until vegetables are soft.
4. Add everything from the saute pan, the pumpkin, and the broth to a blender. Blend until combined.
5. Pour the blended soup into a large stockpot on medium heat, whisk in the coconut milk and then add the bay leaf.
6. Stir often and cook for 15 minutes. Season with salt and pepper to taste. Enjoy, but make sure to remove the bay leaf.

173

Red Potion

Ingredients:
- ¼ cup Sugar
- ¼ cup Water
- 1 Orange, sliced
- 1 Green Apple, sliced
- 1 cup Red Grapes, sliced
- ¼ cup Pomegranate Seeds
- 1 bottle Red Wine
  (or Cranberry Grape Juice)
- 2 cups Pomegranate Juice
- ½ cup Brandy (or Seltzer Water)
- ½ cup Triple Sec
  (or 1 Lemon juiced)

Instructions:
1. Make a simple syrup by mixing the water and sugar in a pot. Bring to a boil and stir well until the sugar is dissolved. Set aside to cool.
2. In a big jar, add simple syrup, fruit, and liquids.
3. Refrigerate for 48 hours and then enjoy. It'll fill up your health bar! No wait, that's just the alcohol. *(If you want more simple syrup, you can easily double the recipe. Just be sure to use equal parts water and sugar.)*

Blue Potion

Ingredients:
-2 oz Blue Curaçao
(or Blue Raspberry Soda)
-2 oz Triple Sec (or Orange Juice)
-Blueberry Lemonade
-1 medium Orange (garnish)
- Ice

Instructions:
1. In a chilled glass, add blue curaçao and triple sec (or blue raspberry soda and orange juice). Add a few pieces of ice and top off the glass with blueberry lemonade.
2. Garnish this powerful drink with a nice, fresh slice of orange.

Chateau Romani

Ingredients:
- 1 cup Sugar
- 1 tbsp Ground Cinnamon
- 1 cup Water
- Maple Syrup
- 2 tbsp Cinnamon Sugar
- 1 cup Ice
- ⅓ cup Milk
- 1 oz Irish Cream Liqueur
  (or Heavy Whipping Cream)
- 1 oz Vanilla Bourbon
  (or 2 tsp Vanilla Extract)
- 1 tbsp Nutmeg
- 1 Cinnamon Stick

Instructions:
Cinnamon Simple Syrup
1. In a small saucepan over medium high heat, combine sugar, cinnamon, and water. Constantly stir until mixture boils. Once boiling, remove from heat and keep stirring until sugar is completely dissolved.

Prepare the Glass
2. On a small plate, add a dollop of maple syrup. Turn your glass or bottle upside down and rub the rim in the maple syrup until it is coated.
3. On a second plate, add the cinnamon sugar. Rub the maple syrup-coated rim in the cinnamon sugar.

Finish and Serve
4. In a cocktail mixer, add ice, milk, Irish cream liqueur (or heavy whipping cream), vanilla bourbon (or vanilla extract), and 1oz of the simple syrup. Shake until the outside of the mixer gets nice and frosty.
5. Pour into your cinnamon rimmed glass and add nutmeg. Stir with a cinnamon stick and experiment with using it as a straw. It's worth a try, at least.

179

Grandma's Soup

Ingredients:
- 2 tbsp Olive Oil
- ½ lb Chorizo
- 1 medium Onion, chopped
- 2 cloves Garlic, minced
- 2 tbsp Cooking Sherry
- 8 cups Chicken Stock
- 4 cups fresh Corn Kernels
- 1 cup Coconut Milk
- 4 ripe Pears, peeled and cubed
- 4 tbsp Cornstarch
- 4 tbsp Cold Water
- Salt and Black Pepper
- 1 tbsp Ground Ginger
- 15 oz can Creamed Corn
- 1 tbsp Apple Cider Vinegar
- 1½ tsp Lime Juice
- ½ tbsp Curry Powder
- 1 tsp Garlic Powder

Instructions:
1. In a large pot, heat olive oil over medium high heat. Add chorizo, stirring occasionally until it starts to brown. Add onion and garlic. Continue to cook until onions are translucent.

2. Deglaze with sherry. Add chicken stock and corn kernels. Bring to a boil, reduce heat to low and simmer for 5 minutes. This is your soup base.

3. In a small pot, add coconut milk and pears on medium heat. Cook until pears are fork tender, about 10 to 15 minutes.

4. Remove mixture from heat, lightly mash the fruit with a fork, and purée in a blender.

5. Add cornstarch to a separate bowl with an equivalent amount of cold water and mix into a slurry. Add the purée and cornstarch mix into the soup base. Bring the soup to a boil.

6. Reduce heat to medium and stir in the remaining ingredients. Simmer for 5 to 10 minutes.

Turtle Rock Cookies

Cake Ingredients:
- 1 cup softened Salted Butter
- 1 cup Sugar
- ½ tbsp Vanilla Extract
- ½ tbsp Almond Extract
- 1 large Egg
- 2 tsp Baking Powder
- 3 cups Flour

Cake Instructions:
1. Preheat oven to 350°F.
2. In a large mixing bowl, cream together butter and sugar, then beat in the egg and both extracts.
3. Mix in baking powder until well incorporated, then add flour.
4. On a floured surface, roll out dough to ¼" thickness.
5. Cut out an equal amount of 1" and 2" circles. Place cookies on a greased baking sheet.
6. Prick holes in your dough with a fork and bake until golden brown, 10 to 13 minutes. Let cookies rest on the sheet for a minute before moving to a cooling rack.

Caramel Ingredients:
- 1 cup Granulated Sugar
- ½ tsp Salt
- ¼ cup Water
- ¼ cup Heavy Cream
- 4 tbsp Butter

Caramel Instructions:
7. In a small saucepan over medium heat, add sugar, salt, and water. Bring to a low boil and stir until dissolved, about 5 minutes.
8. Increase heat to medium-high. Cook without stirring until it starts to look like caramel, about 4 to 5 minutes. *(This is when you should bust out your candy thermometer. Sugar reaches the caramel stage around 350°F. Candy is hard, especially when it's soft.)*
9. Add butter and mix until melted. *(Watch out, the butter will make the caramel bubble up and it is hot! Probably a good idea to wear an apron or a heat-proof tunic on this one.)*
10. Remove from heat and slowly drizzle in heavy cream. Mix well. *(Just like with the butter, the mixture will bubble up so watch out!)*
11. Let cool and transfer to a container. *(You can store it in the fridge. It will keep for a week if you keep it covered. Reheat to make it runny again.)*

Toppings:
- Hazelnuts
- Mini Pretzels
- Sliced Pecans
- Chocolate Chips

Assembly Instructions:
12. Take your 2" cookies and top each one with a small amount of caramel.
13. Put a mini pretzel on top of each cookie, pushing it in a bit so caramel leaks through.
14. Dip a pecan into the caramel, covering it about half way. Place it on the cookie so that hangs over the edge. *(It looks like a little turtle leg!)* Repeat with four more pecans so you have four legs and one head.
15. Add your 1" cookies on top of the pretzel.
16. Melt a handful of chocolate chips in a bowl in the microwave for about 10 seconds. Pour over your cookie to give your little turtles a chocolate 'shell'. *(Don't cover their heads and legs, though!)*
17. Top with a hazelnut slice. *(And maybe add more chocolate.)*

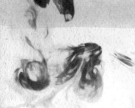

Dark Light Cookies

Cookie Ingredients:
- ½ cup softened Unsalted Butter
- ¼ cup Powdered Sugar
- ½ tsp Vanilla Extract
- A pinch Salt
- 1 cup Flour

Light World Glaze Ingredients:
- 1 cup Powdered Sugar
- 2 tbsp Lemon Juice

Dark World Glaze Ingredients:
- 1 cup Powdered Sugar
- 2 tbsp Blackberries, puréed and strained

Cookie Instructions:

1. Preheat oven to 350°F.

2. In a large mixing bowl, cream together butter and sugar. Add vanilla extract, salt, and flour. Mix until completely incorporated.

3. On a floured surface, roll out dough to ½" thickness. Cut out cookies with a cookie cutter or mason jar lid.

4. Place on a greased baking sheet and bake for 18 to 20 minutes. Set aside to cool.

Glaze Instructions:

5. In separate bowls, mix each set of glaze ingredients until they are of uniform consistency.

6. Use a butter knife to spread the light world glaze over half of each cookie and the dark world glaze over the other half of each cookie.

7. Enjoy the best of both worlds.

Fairy Bomb

Ingredients:
-2 oz Sour Apple Liqueur
(or Green Apple Soda)
-1 oz Vodka (or Seltzer)
-2 oz White Rum
(or Pineapple Juice)
-Ginger Ale
-1 pack Strawberry Pop Rocks
-Edible Glitter

Instructions:
1. In a chilled mug, add sour apple liqueur, vodka, and white rum (or green apple soda, seltzer, and pineapple juice). Fill the rest of the mug about three-fourths of the way full with ginger ale.

2. In a separate shot glass, add a pack of strawberry Pop Rocks and as much edible glitter as you want to ingest *(hopefully not much, if any)*.

3. When you're ready to enjoy this bombastic drink, ensure the area around you is prepared for the flavor explosion *(things might get soaked)*! Drop the shotglass into the mug, say the magic words, and BOOM! FROTHY, BEAUTIFUL, EXPLODY MESS!

WATCH OUT!!

187

Pillowy Roasted Mushrooms

Glaze Ingredients:
- 2 cloves Garlic, minced
- 1 tbsp Fresh Ginger, diced
- 1 Spring Onion, chopped
- 1 tsp Black Sesame Oil
- 2 cups No Pulp Orange Juice
- 2 tbsp Low Sodium Soy Sauce
- 1 tbsp Rice Vinegar
- 1 tsp Orange Zest
- ½ tsp Salt
- ½ cup Honey
- 2 tbsp Cornstarch
- 4 tbsp No Pulp Orange Juice (extra)

Mushroom Ingredients:
- 5 King Oyster Mushrooms, halved
- 1 tbsp Olive Oil
- Red Pepper Flakes (garnish)
- 1 tsp Roasted Sesame Seeds (garnish)

Instructions:
1. Preheat oven to 350°F.
2. Place a pot over medium heat. Once hot, add black sesame oil. Sauté garlic, ginger, and spring onion until browned.
3. Add orange juice, soy sauce, rice vinegar, orange zest, honey, and salt.
4. In a separate pan over medium heat, mix your cornstarch and 4 tbsp orange juice. Stir until thickened, then reduce to low heat and stir occasionally. Leave it on the heat for now. We'll be back, don't worry.
5. Place halved mushrooms on a baking tray lined with parchment paper.
6. Brush mushrooms very lightly with olive oil. *(It is important to not use too much! Mushrooms are very absorbent which means introducing too much liquid will make them soggy.)*
7. Place baking tray in oven and bake for 10 minutes. Remove, flip, and bake for 15 minutes.
8. Once mushrooms are back in the oven, remove orange glaze from heat and set aside.
9. After 15 minutes, flip mushrooms one last time and lightly brush on glaze. Bake for an additional 4 minutes.
10. Plate while hot and go crazy with your glaze and garnish!

189

Kooloolimpah Sundae

Ingredients:

- Vanilla Ice Cream
(use our Elixir recipe)
- 1 tbsp Matcha Powder
- 16 oz Semisweet
Baking Chocolate, chopped
- Small Balloons
(Use red balloons, they'll work better.)
(Trust me.)
- 1 tsp Canola Oil
- Maraschino Cherries
- Sprinkles
- Whipped Cream

Instructions:

1. In a blender, add 1 tbsp of green matcha powder and a few scoops of ice cream. Blend well and place the mixture in the freezer.

2. In a double boiler, melt the chocolate with the canola oil. *(Don't know how to do that? I can walk you through it. Take two pans of roughly the same size and put about 1 to 2 inches of water in the bottom pan. Then put the pan on the stove over medium heat. Place the other pan on top of the first one and add the ingredients you want to melt. Make sure that the bottom of the top pan doesn't touch the water.)*

3. Line a baking sheet with parchment paper and spoon six spoonfuls of melted chocolate on the sheet.

4. Blow up the small balloons, you will be using those balloons to make chocolate bowls so blow them up accordingly. *(We suggest rinsing/washing the balloons before making the bowls.)* Dip the bottom of the balloons into the bowl of melted chocolate to partially coat them, about 3-inches deep. Gently press chocolate covered part of the balloon onto the spoonfuls of chocolate on the baking sheet so they stand upright.

5. Place the baking sheet with the balloons in the freezer for at least one hour.

6. Remove the sheet and balloons from the freezer and poke the balloons with toothpicks to pop them! Gently peel away the popped balloons, leaving behind a chocolate shell shaped like a bowl.

7. *Use our recipe from the glossary to prepare some fresh whipped cream.*

8. Fill your bowl with ice cream, fresh whipped cream, and remaining melted chocolate *(you can reheat it in the microwave for a few seconds so it melts again)*. Top with sprinkles and a maraschino cherry!

9. Enjoy. Tastes so good, you'll wanna eat the bowl!

CHOCOLATE!!! (hot)

CHOCOLATE BOWL?!

191

Rock Brisket

Ingredients:
- 2 tbsp Rock Sugar (or Brown Sugar)
- 2 tbsp Salt
- 2 tbsp Black Pepper
- 2 tbsp Garlic Powder
- 1 tbsp Onion Powder
- 1 tbsp Chili Powder
- 1 tbsp Paprika
- 8 lbs Beef Brisket, chilled
- 1 cup Beef Stock
- ¼ cup Liquid Smoke

Instructions:
1. Preheat the oven to 350°F.
2. In a mixing bowl, mix all the dry spices to create a dry rub. *(Feel free to use more or less, according to your own tastes.)*
3. Remove the brisket from the fridge and trim any silver skin or excess fat. Pat it dry with a paper towel.
4. Coat both sides of the brisket with the dry spice rub. *(Be sure to work it into the meat and really get it in there.)*
5. Put the brisket in a large roasting pan with a rack. Bake for 1 hour.
6. Remove the brisket from the oven briefly to fill the roasting pan with beef stock and liquid smoke. Add additional water so that there's at least ½" of liquid in the roasting pan. Wrap the pan in aluminum foil nice and tight to retain moisture.
7. Lower oven temperature to 300°F and bake for another 3 hours or until tender.
8. Remove the brisket from the oven and allow to rest uncovered on a cutting board for 1 hour before slicing. Cut against the grain and enjoy your tasty meal!

193

Crust Ingredients:
-1 tsp Sea Salt
-½ cup Black Bean Flour
-½ tsp Ground Cayenne
-½ tsp Paprika
-1 tbsp Vegetable Oil
-½ cup Water
-A pinch of Himalayan Pink Salt

Chili Ingredients:
-1 tbsp Olive Oil
-½ cup Onions, chopped
-½ cup Red Bell Pepper, chopped
-3 cloves Garlic, minced
-2 lbs 80/20 Ground Beef
-1 tsp Ground Oregano
-1 tsp Red Pepper Flakes
-1 tbsp Granulated Sugar
-16 oz Tomato Sauce
-2 tbsp Chili Powder
-1 tsp Ground Cumin
-1 tsp Salt
-¼ tsp Ground Cayenne
-1 Jalapeño, diced
-15 oz can Red Beans
-15 oz can Black Beans

Crust Instructions:
1. Preheat oven to 350°F.
2. In a mixing bowl, combine the sea salt, black bean flour, cayenne, and paprika. Add in oil and mix. Slowly mix the water into the batter until slightly runny.
3. Measure the size of the bowl you are using for your chili. On a baking sheet lined with parchment paper, spread a thin layer of the bean paste a little smaller than the diameter of your bowl.
4. Sprinkle a dash of pink sea salt on top of the bean paste and bake for 6 to 10 minutes, until it becomes firm enough to flip. Flip it and then bake for an additional 8 to 10 minutes.

Chili Instructions:
5. Heat olive oil in a large pot over medium high heat, add in onions and bell peppers. Sauté until onions are translucent, about 5 minutes.
6. Add in garlic and cook until fragrant but not browned.
7. Add the ground beef to the pot. Break it apart with a wooden spoon and cook for 6 minutes or until browned, stirring occasionally. Sprinkle in oregano.
8. Add tomato sauce and stir until combined.
9. Add the chili powder, cumin, sugar, salt, pepper, cayenne, red pepper flakes, and jalapeño. Stir well.
10. Strain half the juices from both cans of beans. Add beans along with leftover juices to the pot. Lower heat and simmer for at least 45 minutes.
11. Transfer to a bowl and top with the black bean crust to seal it. Crack open the crust with a spoon and enjoy!

Ingredients:
-8 tsp Hibiscus Flowers, dried
-4 cups Water
-1 tsp Rock Sugar
(or Regular Sugar)
-½ cup Blueberries
-1 cup Lemonade
-1 Lemon
-1 tsp Sugar
-Ice
-2 oz Vodka
(optional)

Hibiscus Potion

Instructions:

1. In a saucepan over medium high heat, add dried hibiscus flowers and 4 cups of water. Stir gently and mix well. Bring to a boil, give it one last gentle stir and remove from heat. Cover and set aside to steep until reduced by half, 8 to 10 minutes.

2. Strain tea into a glass. Add rock sugar and stir to dissolve. Set aside.

3. Purée blueberries and lemonade in a blender on low until smooth. Strain and set aside.

4. In a small dish, zest the lemon and mix with 1 tsp sugar. Juice one half of the lemon into another small dish and set aside.

5. In a cocktail mixer, cover the bottom of the mixer with ice, add 1 cup of hibiscus tea, ½ cup of the blueberry lemonade you had previously set aside, and vodka (optional). Shake well until the outside of the cocktail mixer becomes frosty.

6. Dip the rim of a glass into the lemon juice, then into the lemon zest and sugar mixture.

7. Add ice to your garnished glass and pour the potion over. Add an extra lemon slice and fresh hibiscus flower for garnish.

Fruit and Nut Balls

This recipe was submitted by our dear friend, Hillary Froemel. She's the best!

Instructions:

1. Preheat oven to 350°F.
2. Pulse apricots, figs, coconut, and pumpkin seeds in a food processor until finely chopped.
3. Mix all ingredients together in a mixing bowl, or use your food processor if it's big enough.
4. Roll into roughly 1" balls and place them in a muffin tin. *(This recipe should make about 26 balls, so you might have to bake in multiple batches.)*
5. Bake for 15 minutes. Enjoy while still warm or save for later!

Ingredients:
- ¼ cup Dried Apricots
- ½ cup Dried Black Figs
- ¼ cup Shredded Unsweetened Coconut
- ¼ cup Roasted Pumpkin Seeds
- ¼ cup Flax Seeds
- ¼ cup Hemp Seeds
- ¼ cup Oat Fiber
- 2 tbsp Chia Seeds (optional)
- ¼ tsp Baking Soda
- ¼ cup Olive Oil
- ¼ cup Avocado Oil
- ½ tsp Vanilla Extract
- ¼ cup Granulated Monk Fruit Sweetener
- ¼ cup Monk Fruit Maple Syrup
- 1½ cups Almond Flour

This tasty snack is low carb and great for people on a ketogenic diet!

Italian Pasta Salad

Ingredients:
- ½ cup Extra Virgin Olive Oil
- 2 tbsp Red Wine Vinegar
- 1 tbsp White Wine Vinegar
- 1 tsp Dijon Mustard
- 1/2 tsp Italian Seasoning
- 1 tsp Honey
- 1 tsp Lemon Juice
- Salt and Black Pepper
- 16 oz box Bowtie Pasta
- 12 oz jar Marinated Artichoke Hearts
- 14 oz can Marinated Baby Corn
- 14 oz jar Marinated Hearts of Palm
- 6 oz can Pitted Marinated Black Olives
- ½ cup fresh Grape Tomatoes (optional)
- 12 oz jar Marinated Mushrooms (optional)
- Parmesan Cheese

Instructions:
1. Make your Italian dressing by combining olive oil, vinegars, mustard, Italian seasoning, honey, and lemon juice in a small bowl. Add salt and black pepper to taste and then set aside for later.
2. Cook pasta al dente in a pot of boiling water. Once cooked, drain off the water by pouring into a colander. Rinse under cold water.
3. While boiling pasta, drain and slice all your canned goods (as well as the tomatoes). Combine all sliced items together and drench with your Italian dressing to taste.
4. Combine sliced goods with pasta and mix well, adding a little more dressing. Top with a sprinkling of parmesan and then cover and refrigerate until chilled (at least 2 hours).
5. Serve chilled, maybe add some more dressing before serving.
6. Might as well add more dressing.

Simple Rice Balls

This recipe was submitted by Lucky Hand Dice.
Disclaimer: This recipe is brought to you by my hungry child so there are no exact measurements. Good luck!

Instructions:

1. Make some steamed rice (use our recipe from the glossary).

2. Scoop out some warm rice and, while it's still warm, add about a tablespoon of vinegar and mix together.

3. Sprinkle in your favorite sweetener. I use honey powder, but you can use sugar or honey. The sweetness should balance out the vinegar.

4. Then add a salt. I use a Korean beef stock, but you can use anything that is salty like miso or... ya know, salt...

5. Sprinkle in some sesame seeds and mix well. Make sure to taste and add additional seasoning if needed.

6. Grab a bunch of your now-seasoned rice and compress into a ball. Take some nori seaweed and gently press it onto one side of the ball until it sticks. This will be your handle so you can eat it without getting your fingers sticky!

7. Set them on a plate and add a few more sesame seeds on top. Done!

8. Good to be set out, but covered, for 4-7 hours at room temperature. Great for hungry babies!

Ingredients:

- Some Steamed Rice
- Vinegar
- Honey Powder
  (or your sweetener of choice)
- Korean Beef Stock, Miso or Salt
- Sesame Seeds
- Nori Seaweed

Ted's Hazelnut Parsnip Soup

Ingredients:
- 1 Squash (Acorn or Butternut)
- Extra Virgin Olive Oil
- 2 tbsp Sesame Oil
- 2 tbsp Butter
- 2 cups Button Mushrooms, chopped
- 3 cloves Garlic, minced
- 1 whole Leek, chopped
- 3 Green Onions, chopped
- 4 Shallots, chopped
- 5 cups Vegetable Broth
- 3 Parsnips, peeled and chopped
- 1½ cups Hazelnuts, chopped
- 1 tsp Thyme
- 1 tsp Sage
- 2 tbsp Rosemary
- ½ cup Heavy Cream
- Salt and Black Pepper

Squash Instructions:
1. Preheat oven to 350°F.
2. Spread the chopped hazelnuts out evenly on a parchment paper covered baking sheet.
3. Bake hazelnuts for 5 minutes, remove and set aside.
4. Increase the oven temperature to 400°F and coat a baking sheet with cooking spray.
5. Prep the squash by cutting the entire thing lengthwise and lightly coat the flesh with olive oil. Sprinkle with sage, salt and pepper.
6. Place squash on the sprayed baking sheet skin side down and roast until fork tender, 35 to 45 minutes.

Soup Instructions:
7. In a large pot, melt butter over low heat. Saute the vegetables starting with the mushrooms.
8. After 5 minutes, add garlic and sesame oil.
9. After another 2 minutes add the leeks, shallots and onions. Saute for a final time until the leeks and onions are caramelized, 10 to 15 minutes.
10. Add the vegetable broth and deglaze the pan.
11. Add the parsnips and ¾ of the hazelnuts (reserving ¼ for garnish). Season with thyme, salt, and pepper to taste.
12. Bring to a boil, then reduce the heat and simmer 20 minutes, covered.

Assembly:
13. Scoop out the flesh of the squash and add it to the broth.
14. Use an immersion hand blender to smooth the soup, and, if desired, strain through a sieve until silky smooth. Alternatively, work in batches to purée the soup in a blender and recombine.
15. Once smooth, add heavy cream and rosemary over low heat. Taste and add additionals spices to your liking. Garnish with hazelnuts.
16. Share with someone you love.

This recipe was submitted by Joey as a wedding present for Ted. Congratulations! <3

Mighty Bananas Foster

Instructions:

1. In a large skillet, heat the butter and allow it to melt over medium heat.

2. Add quartered bananas and allow them to brown on the flat side.

3. Add brown sugar (not directly on top of bananas) and allow it to melt without stirring. Deglaze skillet with alcohol away from the heat. *DO NOT DO THIS NEAR AN OPEN FLAME!*

4. This next step is pretty dangerous so be careful. You don't even have to do this but if you do, make sure you do it in an open area, away from other flammable elements, and have a fire extinguisher on hand because your skillet is about to burst into flames. Place the skillet back on the heat and ignite the alcohol with your long match and *WATCH OUT.*

5. *Don't panic.* The fire will die down once the alcohol has burned off. Once the flames have died, add spices and squeeze an orange slice over the top.

6. Remove from heat and serve immediately over ice cream.

Ingredients:
- 1 Long Match
- 2 tbsp Unsalted Butter
- ½ cup Brown Sugar
- 2 Bananas, quartered
- ½ tsp Ground Cinnamon
- ½ tsp Ground Nutmeg
- ¼ cup Brandy, Cognac, or Rum (optional)
- Orange, sliced
- A pinch of Salt
- Your Favorite Ice Cream

EXPERT RECIPE! BE CAREFUL AND HAVE A FIRE EXTINGUISHER ON HAND!

This recipe was submitted by our dear friends Wayne and Joseph Eggert.

Seasoned Butter Ingredients:
-6 tbsp Unsalted Butter, room temperature
-1 tbsp Rosemary, chopped
-1 tbsp Thyme, chopped
-1 tbsp Chives, chopped

Brine Ingredients:
-1 gallon Water
-2 cups Kosher salt
-2 tbsp Black Peppercorns
-1 tbsp Whole Allspice
-2 tbsp Whole Cloves
-2 Bay Leaves, crumbled
-1 Onion, chopped
-1 Carrot, chopped
-1 stalk Celery, chopped with leaves
-1 large Chicken
-2 quarts Ice

Final Preparation:
-Brined Chicken
-Seasoned Butter
-2 tbsp Salt
-2 tbsp Black Pepper
-2 tbsp Olive Oil
-Kitchen Twine

Whole Roasted Cucco

Seasoned Butter Instructions:
1. Mix all ingredients together and form into two equal, thin disks. The disks need to be thin so they can be slipped under the skin of the chicken without tearing it.
2. Store in refrigerator for at least 30 minutes.

Brine Instructions:
3. Add the salt, spices, onion, carrot, and celery to a gallon of water and bring to a boil.
4. Cut off heat once it has began to boil and let sit until room temperature. Once the brine is at room temperature, pour the mixture over your ice and then place a whole chicken in the ice bath.
5. Allow to brine for 2-4 hours in the refrigerator. Then remove chicken from brine solution.

Final Instructions:
6. Preheat oven to 375° F.
7. Lay chicken breast up in a pan on a wire rack and carefully slide thin seasoned butter disks under the skin of each breast.
8. Heavily salt and pepper the entire bird.
9. Cut about three feet of kitchen twine.
10. Start to tie up the bird by placing the center of the twine below the tailbone of the bottom of the bird.
11. Take each end of the twine and wrap it around the bottom of the corresponding leg, then cross the two ends of twine in the middle to pull the two legs together.
12. Once the legs are tight and secure, pull the two ends of the twine up the chicken's body. Pin the wings tightly to the side of the body.
13. Continue pulling the twine ends up to the neck area and crisscross them over the neck hole. Sinch it tight and knot it off. Cut excess twine.
14. Coat in olive oil and bake for 1 hour and 15 minutes til cooked completely.
15. Carve that bird up!

This recipe was submitted by our dear friends Wayne and Joseph Eggert.

-Li Kovács @LiKovacs

We Love Our Artists

The artists involved in this cookbook are incredibly talented individuals who really brought this book to life. We're gonna take a few pages to showcase their best work. Find them on social media and give them lots of love for everything they do!

Bianca Perez @SparklingAmphy

Ari Prokos / @arriticus

シLV / @borzoieyes

Marco Fedele / @TheMarcotto

Fred Brown / @bredfrown

Erin Ong / @erintheozian

Bianca Perez / @SparklingAmphy

Margeaux McClelland / @MargeauxDesign

Camila Inoa / @camiinoa

Erin Ong / @erintheozian

Camila Inoa / @camiinoa

ケレ∨ / @borzoieyes

Emma M / @magypsyparty

Kelly Pringle / @plantjuice

Marco Fedele / @TheMarcotto

Emma M / @magypsyparty

Fred Brown / @bredfrown

Morgan / @Incogneko

Alyssa Browning / @kiddytank

Kelly Pringle / @plantjuice

Morgan / @Incogneko

Ari Prokos / @arriticus

Alyssa Browning / @kiddytank

Madi / @spacediscos

Madi / @spacediscos

Credits

ᔑᒷ ᓵᑑᗢᒣᒲᒷ ᑑ ᒷᓭ ᔑᒷ ᒣ

Peter J. Abreu - Lead Chef, Manager, Artist
Matthew Mannheimer - Social Media, PR Manager
Alyssa Browning - Sous-chef, Artist
Hillary Froemel - Writer
Patrick Deasy - Photographer, Videographer
Emma M. - Assistant Producer, Artist
Casey Corrigan - Editor
ケLV - Artist
Kelly Kirsch - Artist
Margeaux McClelland - Cover Artist
Josette Abreu - Best Mom, Assistant Chef

Camila Inoa - Artist
Marco Fedele - Italian, Artist
Fred Brown - Graphic Designer
Erin Ong - Artist
Bianca Perez - Artist
Morgan - Artist
Madi - Artist
Li Kovács - Vista Artist
Ari Prokos - Artist
JobJob LLC - Publishing Company

Special Thanks

-GENKI (Buy their Dongle!)
-Alakazam3000 (Editing Machine)
-The Yetee (Hi Glen and Mike)
-Jacob (Thanks for the Pepper)
-Zelda Dungeon and Zelda Informer

-Tiny Miss-Fromage
-Lindsey Butler (<3)
-Rose Jackson (Edits!)
-Zelda Universe
-Kotaku Australia

-Alex Trevino
-Austin O'Rourke (Music King)
-Reb Valentine (Editing Wizard)
-Kickstarter (and Backers!)
-Our Amazing Discord Community!

Backer Credits

Hillary Froemel

Valarie Rock

Spiraling Helix
(AJ Merrigan)

Benjamin Winstead

Lucky Hand Dice

Nick Johnston

Rinubus

Joseph and Ted

weirdguy42

MandarTheMousey

Megan Drummond  Lucio Blanco  Megan Cantwell Rhea Mac

Josette Abreu
(Mom)

Luis Coria

Jake Harris

Heidi Ruff

Collin Ice   Triplicate Entertainment   Josh and Jordan

Jop   Joooo₀₅   Gavin McGrew   David Anderson

Jackson LaDuke   Katlin Spangler   Neressa Salazar   Piper Thunstrom

 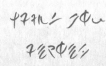

Jörg Tragert   Richard Ervin Jr

211

@monster_battle
4444
9th Chap
A backer
a friendly culinary adventurer
A lover of food and fiction
A passionate cook
A yellow rupee
A. A. MacConnell
A. Williams
Aaron Jacobson
Aaron Stabbert
Aaron, Lisa, & Elizabeth Caress
A-C Duroi
Adam Brewer
Adam Bullmer
Adam Debter
Adam K.
Adam M. Carner - Shoreline, CT - Viperboy749
Adam P
Adam Salvador-Hernandez
Adam Vickerman
Adam Weinstein
Adam Zolan
Adventurer Robin
Agadez
Aidan Isaacson
Aiden "Why Did I Find 1800 Korok Seeds" McGrath
AKB
akimika
Alan Hartings
Alaura
Aleb
Alec Cohan
Alethel
Alex Franco Silva
Alex Heinrichs
Alex Vanover
Alex Wood
Alexander Beech
Alexander Hershel
Alexander Kohl
Alexandre Abrao
AlexFex
Alexis S. Anderson
Alia bt. Ghazaime
Aline-Claire Huynh
Alisha Jones
Alison Ivey
Allan Silva
Allie
Allison and Tyler Huffman
Ally Boice
Ally Crooks
Alyssa "Kay" Mibb
Alyssa Lane
Amanda Hingston
Amanda Koller
Amanda Obodovsky
Amanda VanHiel

Amanda Winters
Amber Wyss
Amelia Rose
Amerlyn Zeta
Amilia Anton
Amoeba Bait
Amy Driedger
Amy F.
Amy Hotz
Amy K
Suzanne Parent
Benjamin "Spice" Winstead
Ana Herrera
Anders "burns water" Nilsson
Andrea "XFox" Govoni
Andrea C. DePaula
Andrea Dworkowski
Andrea Huswan
Andrea Jaramillo
Andrea Klenner
Andreas "Skaw" Maurer
Andrew (Spiralling Helix) Merrigan
Andrew Hovanec
Andy Knight
Angel, Donnie, and Nathan <3
Anna Ball
Anna Levinson, wielder of the blade.
Annalisa The Purple Girl
Anne
Anonymous Chef
AntDude
Anthony Godfrey
Anthony Gonzalez
Anthony Wastella
Antoine AUTHIER
Antonio Notte
Aoife Simpson
Apothecary Caldwell
arathaur
Arazien
Arcane Arts
Aretsuya
Ari Miller
Ariëlla F. Reinders
Aristides Flores
Arleen Silvero
Arno en Mirjam
Arvin Chlochaisri
aryxenys
As a proud Supporter of the cook book
Ash Force
Ash Novreske
Ash Yee
Ashe Cosme please and thank you!!
Ashleigh Green
Ashleigh Larkin
Ashley Roberts
Ashley Ruffini
Ashley Stovell

Asm
Asya from Moscow
Athena Costilow
Audrey Kare
Aunt Chiche
Austin [ValantWynn]
Austin Crawford
Austin David
Austin J. Kukay
Austin Kohagen
Autumn Beauchesne
Autumn G. Van Kirk
Avery M.
Avinash Nooka
Avril
awesome and wise southerner
Aya
Ayden Castellanos
Azuzuzuli
B Langford
Backer
Bader Z.
Bailey and William Hayes
Bailey krebz
Barkingbeagle
Baron Van Pinxteren
Becca Parker
Beef Hamstring
Ben and Rachel M.
Ben B
Ben Newell
Ben Pauze
Benedict Robinson
Benjamin "Baltor" B.
Benjamin E Miller
Benjamin Juan
Benjamin Spirason
Berke C.
Bernz182
Beth
Bianca Perez
Bill Swarmer
Billy Hall III
Blake Brogden
BlockHead Gaming
Bob Covey
Bobby Cook
Bobby Keller
boenzlip
Bonnie Fitzgerald
Brady Suttles
Brady Zwick
Brandon & Ren Jett
Brandon Babcock
Brandon Cossaboon
Brandon Greathouse
Brandon Hewes
Brandon Pollick
Brandon Rodriguez
Brannon
Brave New World
Bravo Peperoncini
Brenda Fellman

Brennan James Donnell ("Boots")
Breton
Brian & Vidhya LaMoreaux
Brian A
Brian and Supaporn Winterberg
Brian McLaughlin
Brian Simmons
Briana Weiss
Briana Weiss
Brien Tennefoss
Bright Chen
Brinton
Britney Lee Bowers
Britni Ely
Britt Hart
Brittany C
Brittany S.
Britton Hipple
Brockston Lewis
brokenpetridish
Bruce.erq
Bryan Smith Jr.
Bullmaster
Bvo
Caitlin Jane Hughes
Caitlin Johnson (Sage of Hyrule)
Caitlin Richardson
Caleb B. Hitz
Caleb Carvell
Callieopes
Cam Schmitt
Cameron Foley
Cameron T. Reeves
Camilla Ballinger
Candice Lee (BellusOddities)
Cap
Captain Dibbzy
Captain Theo
Captain Tidus Maxamilian
Cara Ficocelli
Carlo DeSantis
Carola Tobar
Carolyn Doerr
Carson Clement
Caryl F
Casey F.
Cassandra Frisch
Cassie Jo
Cassy Shaw
Cath Nils
Catherine
Catherine Harvey
Cauchemar
Cece & Thor Thomas
Cecily R. Tavares
Chana C.
Chandler Hubbard
Chas Leese
chase McKinney
ChefBoyardank
Chelsea Beam
Chelsey Greene
Chemin Chow
Cherie Davidson

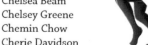

Chestnut
Cheyenne Fox
Chibi Okamiko
Chloe Gray
Chloe Rain Booth
Chris Belcher
Chris Boulton
Chris C
Chris C
Chris C Liu
Chris Hanlon
Chris Smith
Chris Welsh
Christian Fuchs
Christian Hickey
Christian Rosas
Christian Sandell
Christophe Bellangeon
Christopher Bulux
Christopher Luciano Chaidez
Chuck Hewitt
Cindy Tang
Cippi & Bubi
Circe
Claire Shaw
Claudia Villeneuve
Claudio S
Cleonic
Clouds
CNM
Cody "Poot" Davis
Cody Alcina
Cole Flinn
Colleen K. Mallon
Collin Ice
CompanionToBe
Connie M.
Conor Tanji
Corben Crites
Corby aka Lunar Legend
Corbyn Harris
Cordelia "Midna" S
Corwynn Haven
Courtney S.
CptnAlex
CptnMarVill :)
Crisselixir!
Cristoffer Westerström
Crystal Lanzana
CutieCatQueen
D. William Patton, Esq.
Daan "NintenDaan" Koopman
Dabombster
Dafne d'Esposito
dalvenjah
Dalya Scop
Damien S.
Dan "Captain" Howard
Dan & Alanna Furst
Dana
Dana I.
Dani Reichman
Daniel Edwards

Daniel Gousset
Daniel H.
Daniel Pisani
Daniel Pisani
Daniel Quintero
Daniel Rådberg
Daniel Willis
Daniel Winsor
Danielle Van Hecke
Danny Garant
Danny Lightning
Dante & Atari
Daphne Deadwood
Darren Lewis
Dave Kirk
Dave Menor Jr
Dave Williams
Davey & Gwen
David
David & Jennifer Armstrong
David & Lori
David Anderson
David Brännström
David Goyzueta
David Hoeppner
David Nystrom
David Ruskin
David Zazzo
Davide Link Cenzi
DavideM - NoNoSiCerto
Dean Windemuller
Dean Wood
Deborah A. Flores
Dee and Ken
Deinos Molina (Demix)
Delmer Fry
Delta S
Devin Rogers
Devon Martin
Dimitri Anesti
Dimitri Bouniol
Dirk-Jan Mulders
dixson.zhu@gmail.com
Dizzy Bullock
DJ Rose
Doc Blue
Dominick Scarola
Donahue-Grayhek Family
Donna Phonsane
Donovan A. DiPasquale
Dorina Dincklage
Dottie G
Dr Mystic
Dr. R
Dr.Kathy
Draccel
Drew Richardson
DrkNghtSky
Dukey
Duncan
Dustin Beard
Dylan
Dylan Arabie

Dylan L. King
E. & S. Gregg
E. Phillips
Eden & Lest
Edison Wang
Edme Amerigo
Edward B
Elaine P.
Electricmareeps
Eleesana
Elegion
Elena Theres
Elessar Arnold
Eliot Nelson
Elisabeth Keeney
Elizabeth Ansley
Elizabeth C. Perry
Elizabeth Rivera
Elliot Eversdijk
Elliott
Elliott I Davis
ElPolloLoco391
Em Grayson
Emanuel DePaz
Emerald Green Falcon
Emi LinXiao
Emiliano Aguilar Niebla
Emily "Ellian" Smith
Emily Chevalier
Emily Cooper
Emily Jablonski
Emily Kutchins
Emily Mosher
Emily Russell
Emma Roberts
Emma Varney
EPK & SWS
Eric
Eric "Moonbird" Luna Falcon
Eric Schulzetenberg
Eric Torres
Erica B and Todd E
Erica Nation
Erika DiTomaso
Erin Butler
Erin Ferguson
Erin Harker
Erin McIntyre
eskimo777
Ethan
Eugene Schmitz and Cassie Schmitz
Eugene Tan
Evan Rion
Evan Shininger
Faisal Murad
FantQuarTZ
Fatima Khalid
Felicia Gilcris
Felix Sanchez Klose
fellow adventurer? I dont know.
Ffion Jayne Coomber
For Magnus

For Tanner, may you become as skilled in cooking as Link. -Nick Thompson
Forgott3nToast
Forstle
Frances Browne
Fred & Susan Mannheimer
Frederick Leidl
Friend and supporter
Friendly contributor
Frosttoys
fujita
Gabriella Romagnuolo & Eric Woodring
Gabby Goff
Gabriel Interiano
Gabriele De Cagna
Gabrielle Hughes
Gabrielle Winterton
GalacticAttorney
Ganikus
Garrett Kemp
Gavin McGrew
Gavin Storey
Gawdho
GazonArtificiel
Genki
Geoff (Hunter,Killian)
Geoffrey "Copperdragon" Clark
George K
GERUDOKU
Ghostbane
Gift for my 3rd born, a super fan
Gillian Streeter
Gin
Giselle Vadam
Giulia Scaltriti
Gladhwen
GlitchxCity
Glitterbooger
Gloomy Aardvark
Gnoffo Bardoffi
gnuwarchief
Goddess Hylia
Gordhan Rajani
Gordon Stephen
gordoniankid
Grace P.
Grace Vorosmarti
Graham "TheGameboyGTS" Davenport
Grayson Bosworth
Grimd0rk
Grizz
Guaty
Gustavo Aburto
Gwendolyn R. Schmidt
gwenjen10
Haitani
Haitao Huang
Haley Cable
Haley McCarthy
Hanna Zimpfer

Hannah Gibson
Hannah Stevens
Hannelore Nistor
Hans Hagen
Hawk Smith
hayesjuliec@yahoo.com
Haylee Huddleston
Haze Conqueror of Fantasy Food
Hazymoonz
Heather D
Heather Heim
Heidi Ruff
Heiko Schmidt
Helen Febrie
Herbert R. Castillo F.
HeroIne95
Hester Hoyle
Hillary (Bee) Froemel
Hiro Ng
Hogyoku Cosplay
Homesilvercraft
Hong Zhi Zhu
Huxley Rose Ross
Hyper Potions
Hyrule's #1 Potato Farmer
I would prefer not to be, thank you. :)
Ian G Bunn
Ian Roseman
icephoenix
Ichino
ig @tetracos
Indie Contreras
International chef Michael Gebauer
Irene MG
Isaac K. Thompson
Isaac Wurmbrand
Isis E. Prosser
Itzal Mallory
Ivan Leibbrandt
iylila
Izzy Novada
J Sherman
J. Curtis
J.E. Ruiz
j.vingback@gmail.com
J12kon
Jack and Evelyn Currie
Jack Moon
Jack Stahl and Crinni Cooper
Jackie "999 Korok Seed" Stotlar
Jackie A. Rossi
Jackie Johnson
Jackson "Crowbird" LaDuke
Jacob "Verxl" Sedloff
Jacob Evans
Jacob Gill
Jacob Hobbie
Jacob Holte
Jacob Jewson
Jacob Loukota
Jacob Munro

Jacobo Hernández – The Potato Violin
Jade Nielsen
Jake "McHaffie" Harris
Jake Adkins
Jake D Osborne
James "AuriJames" Ford
James 'Jacko' Jackson
James Cousett
James Kilpatrick
James M Harries
Jameson 'JOGURT' Sutton
Janai Lorrin
Jared Hays
Jared Spotts
Jas Husson
Jasef & Leanna Wisener
Jasmine Ib
Jason & Kelsey Frye
Jason Choi
Jay
Jay's Mother Cluckers
JBHarvey
jDoe
Jeanette Volintine
jed176
Jeff and Sarah!
Jeffrey D Sherman
Jenn Dolari
Jenna Hamilton
Jenni T.
Jennie Strunk
Jennifer Hayes
Jennifer Johnson
Jennifer Layla
Jennifer Seay
Jennifer Warren
Jenny Oehlert
Jeremy Kowalski
Jess Dulin
Jess Platter
Jessa & Alec Deaubl
Jesse Parra
Jessica "Linxzie" Whiting
Jessica Berry
Jessica Furtado
Jessica Greene
Jessica McGinnis
Jessica Scott
Jessica Townsend
Jessica Welke-Schaeffer
Jessie D Reno
Jesus
Jezbel3315
Jill & Jordan Atkins
Jill Theresa
Jill Wong @TheMotleyGeek
Jimmy, Kali, Jenni, and Seamus Quinlivan
JJ Lee
jlbauer2@asu.edu
Jo F
Joan

Joanna Wong
Jocelyn *Cabbit* Gorman
Joe Lunsford
Joe Phillips
Joel R. Agruso
Joel 'Thorward' Lajeunesse
Joey Levin and Ted Schevey
Joey spratt
Johan Kuitunen
Johann Alexander
John Browne
John Christian Dolan
John Cmar
John DeKlein
John Hobkinson
John Nguyen
JoJo
Joker
Jon Jones
Jon Lett, Lifetime Zelda Fan
Jonathan Berger
Jonathan Markowski
Jonathan Ritacco
Jonathan van der Meulen
JoodallyJoo
Joooo
Jop Peeters
Jordan Cabe
Jordan Laidlow
Jordan M
Jordan S
Jörg Tragert
Jori Walton
Jose "NeoAnthony" Montes
José Eduardo "churrasquito con arroz" Alvarez
Jose Manuel Franco
José Pablo Parajeles
Jose Serrano
Joseph A Micali III
Joseph De Maria
Joseph Letavis
Joseph Snell
Josette Abreu
Josh "Juice" Jones
Josh Browning
Josh D.
Josh Donnelly
Josh Wein
Joshua Chacona
Joshua Huffman
Joshua Kalms
Joshua Lake
Joshua Sinnett
Josline Phoon
JT Gryder
Juan Hernandez
Julia "RheaKat" Kent
Julia Chateauvieux
Julian D
Julien Clemmen
Justin and Leslie Jacobson-"Dice and Zelda"
Judy Ann Calder

Justin Gilbert
Justin Mahin
Justin Mitchell
Justin Pavesi
Justin Spencer
K & K Schalin
K Strzelecki
K. X. Douglas
K.E. Clausen
K2
Kaalina
Kaelley Bruce
Kai and Bee
Kaitlin Spangler, Coffee Mage
kaitokaito
Kalábovi
Kamron Reimer
Kara Roncin & James Wheeler
Karen Gladstone
Karen Zhou
Karilink
Karsten König
Kashmir Mikos
Kat
Kat Tobias
Kate Brown
Kate Paisley
Katherine Knight
Katherine S
Katherine Swanson
Kathryn Flucht
Katie Berntson and Phil Konecky
Katie Frederick
Katie Horgen
Katie S
Katie Silvernail
Katrina Pecina
Katy "Jetrics" Latham
Kaydee Radovcich
Kaydee Stratford
Kayla Birrittier
Kayla Hadley
KayLynn Owens Murrell
Kaytee Pappas
Kazair Lux
KC Shadow
Keaton Bui
Keenan Loughery
Keith Stanley
Keldi
Kellen Casem
Kelly Bell
Kelly Knox
Kelly Lockwood
Kelsey Christen
Kelsey E. Phillips
Kelsey Morgan
Kelsie Turner
Kelvin Rios (Epic Gamer)
Kendall W
Kennedy Parker
Kenneth Bell
Kenneth Zabielski

Fennel

Kenneth Zidek
Kenny Martin
Kenzie Nokomis
Kerry Klein
Kevin A. Jimenez
Kevin Tang
Kiana Robinson
Kieran Simpson
Kieron Stoff
Kierra Mickey
Kilsguardian
Kimberly Schmidt
King Heiple
Kinsey Underbrink - Happy 30th Birthday
Kirby Morris
Kirielu
Kita SDS
KitKat V
Kitsune Kianya Fireweed of the Northwestern Arctic Borough
Kindred
KJ Williams - Triptych LCA
Klemetti
klinkit
koilantern
Kornelius Haddal Røssevold
Kortney Kropp
Krem Al-Anzi
Kris Kannel
Kristen P
Kristian Handberg
Kristin Morin
Kristina M. Joseph
Kristy, Zach and Sammy Smith
Krys Ali Cordoba
Krystal P.
Kurtis Rodine
Kwadwo Gray
Kyle Anderson
Kyle Gardner-Palmer
Kyle Groom
Kylie Graham
Lacey Nicole Steele
Lady Cerebellum
LadyLycami
Lai Ling Ling
Lamb
Laura Rhodes
Laurel Gangloff
Lauren Banks
Lauren F. Ignacio
Lauren Lacera
Lauren M
Lauren McLemore
Laurens Wolf
Lawjick
lazerem
Leah and Emilio
Leah Braukman
Leah Soll
Leahlostheart
Lee Marsh

Lee Starling
Lee Sugimoto
Legend of Zelda fan
legendoflane
Lemon Kinty
Lena Smith
LesleyDawn
lewisrockets
Lexi
Lexie Green
Leyla Aydin
Lhethi
Lida Supernaw
Likeablespoon47
Lilith
Lina Norring
Linas
Linda A. Daves and Edward J. Falkenstein IV
Lindsay Robinson
Lindsey Butler
Lindsey K
Linkobrata
Linksliltri4ce
Linktober (Joel Siegel)
Linus Freund
Lisa Salvesen
Litamaco
LittleJennyWren
LittleZbot
Liv G
lixiaopei
Lo
Lola de Roon
LordRoto
Lorelei Blackwell
Loren McCoy
LoruleanHeart
Louis-Philippe Fortin
Lovenji
Luca Sergio
Lucky Hand Dice
Lucy Belle Guthrie
Luffy M.
Luis Coria "Hillexia"
Luís Illingworth
Luis Prata
Lukas Feinweber
Lukas Klapatch
Luke and Jennifer Kraft
Luke Francis Muller
Luke Maes
Luke Tammadge
Luke Wheeler
M Silvén
M.E.L
M.J. Reed
MacKenzie Bolek
maddie
maddy :0
Maddy Nerdin
Madeleine Horner
Madison Howell

Madulun
Magne Dyrnes
Magolor Mudkip
Mai8a
Maisy Kay
Mal Prue
Mandar Mousey
Mandy Kuehn
Mandy Wilkerson
Maniac Mayhem
Manuel Reche
Mar Soulstar
Marc "Maniac"
Marc-Anthony Espinoza
Marcel "madjo" de Jong
Marceline Errera
Marco Fedele
Marco Mendoza
Marco Ombri
Marcus Funke
Margaret St. John
Maria Payan-Perkowski
María Solá Laguens
Mariah Griffin
Marie Terskikh
Marilyn "Rhiannon" K.
Mark Robinson
Marky Di Dür
MartDiamond
Martin Buschmann Rustan
Martina Schwerdtfeger
Marty McCarthy
Mary Gerace
Mary Stowe
Marzipans
mashedpopoto
Mathias
Mathias Bourgoin
Mathias.le
Matthew "Watz" Campbell
Matthew "Мат" Chow
Matthew Allen
Matthew Bonnema
Matthew Decker
Matthew Fencil
Matthew Lusk "mbArcher"
Matthew Taranto (BitF)
Max Ferraro
Max Humphries
May B.
Maya
Maya Sternberg
Maynic
McKenna Krebs
McKenzie Wood-Rich
Meagan Pothoven
Meepsworth
Meg
Megan & Matthew Russell
Megan Cantwell
Megan D
Megan Drummond
Megan M O'Callaghan

Meghan
Megz Cantara
Mei-SunHyun
Melanie Munro
Melinda Yin
Melissa Cash
Melissa E.M.
Melissa M.C.
Melissa Mistress of Music
Mellando
Meredith Hannaway
MetaverseNomad
Micaela\@cryosphinx
Micah King
Michael "Chrnomage" Ng
Michael Creech
Michael Douglas
Michael Eric Ray Williams
Michael Garrett Holcombe
Michaël Guérette
Michael Lam
Michael Leonardo
Michael van Rhee
Michel Boutros
Michelle Fore
Michelle Hastings
Michelle McCurdy and Matthew J. Smith
Michelle Townsend
Michole Miller
Miguel Angel Rocha Jr.
Miguel Monterrubio
Mikael Hansson
Mike "Game and" Deitz
Mike Furst
Mike Gergar
Mike S.
Milen S
Milo Mocha
Min
Mindie J. Simmons
Mint of the Twilight
Miranda M.
Miriah & Jay
MischaCrossing
Miss Katie May
Miss-Fromage
Mochaqt
Modjeska Hutchings
MoJo
Monica - Hylian Homemaker
Monica Calvert
Monica power
Monika Zins
Montana
Morgan & Rob Kostelnik
Morgan Ferruccio
Morgan Stitt's Mum and Dad
Mox
Mr Kronus
Mr. & Mrs. Rentner
Mr.Dr.Pib
Mr.Scratch

MrJuanUp
Ms. Adrienne Holt
MudkipGames258
Mycah Duran
MykonosFan
Myles Tesdahl
MythicPhoenix
Myu
N. Kim
N. Maaß
N/A
Na
Nadia Heller
Nahomi-Clyde :)
NajaSide
Nancy Shaw
Nanolx
Natalie Cooper
Nathan Penland
Nathan Weller
Nathaniel Yourgans
Nathen Griffiths
Nattho
Neal Whittle
NeikeDjour
Neil Tekamp
Nenyi Mills-Robertson
Neon
Nestor Pumilio
Nevturiel
Nia W.
Nicholas Altizer
Nicholas Cecil Hatcher
Nicholas Fiorentini
Nick "Raglan" Johnston
Nick Czerew
Nick Dillon
Nick Johnston
Nick T.
Nick Tsakir
Nick Woodring
Nicki K.
Nicolas Cortez
Nicole
Niki Coppola
Nikki Jeske
Nikkori Love
Nina Tungjairob and Armaun
Mirshamasi
NintendoJake
NLdemo
No
No credit
No credit, please.
Noah Cleveland
Noralie
NotEnoughCheese
notPlayer1
Núria G. A.
Nya Tsudha
Oliver B.
Olivia Coffin & Sam Clark
Omar Mazin

omega_entity
Orin
Oscar G
Oscar Maciel Castillo
OtakuNerdGirl
Owen Sotak
Paige Luther
Paige Olivia
Pam Virtucio
Pamela S.
Pan D MacCauley
Patricia R. Fox
Patrick B Hatleberg
Patrick Hawes-DeFrias
Patrick Kercher
Patrick P.
Patrick Schmeichel
Paul "Alakazam3000" Gordon
Paul "We Can Pickle That" Widdel
Paul Fletcher
Paul L. St-Jean
Paul Maranski
Paul Palumbo
Paul X. Flanagan
Paulina Roura
Peppermint Bubble
Percy
Per-Philip Sollin
Peter Stockwell (pwlas)
Petrea Boning
Pez Amaury
Philip Curcuru IV
Philip Ehrenberg
Philip Michael Ferraro-long live
Sherlock hound and the greatest
of luck on your amazing book
peter you rock!
Philip Reed
PhoenixBlade
PikachuKing
Pindar
PinkieOats
Piper Thunstrom
Pippa Brown
Pitayo San
Pixeliz
Professor Shyguy
Przemysław Wójcik
Pudgy Budgie
Quincy King II
R.M. Roberts
Rachael "Not-So-Legendary Chef"
Passov
Rachael M
Rachael MacLeod
Rachael Perkins
Rachael R.
Rachel and Tab
Rachel Kallio
Rachel Kimberly Hastings
Rachel Lurie
Rachel Mackenzie
Rachel Sim

Rafal Frelas
Rairix
Ralle
Rami the Chihuahua
Rancho Tejana
Raphael
"KatanaBeatsPaper"Magalong
Raphaël Mathieu (Linkraph1)
Rasmus Hemmingsen
Raymond C.
Rebecca Baubé and Gracie Setzler
Rebecca Beimers
Rebecca Rudranath
Rebeccah Swanson
recipes
RedSaber23
Regina Matke
regnis3
Rei Pennington
Reikane (Renee)
Remington Pollock
René Zmugg
Renée Adams
RetroRoyaleStudios
RetroStebbson
Reverse Goth Flipper
Rhea Mac
Rhel ná DecVandé
Rhiannon Riesenmy
Ricardo Espinoza Jr.
Ricardo Franco Jr
Richard "Damoncord" Rudel Jr
Richard + Jennifer Berthelot
Richard Ervin Jr.
Ricky Mooney
Robby Trail
Robert and Krystal Johnson
Robert Dewald
Robert F
Robert Sankar
Robert Zollo
Roberto "Berto" Enriquez
Robin, Maker of Things
Roderick Chang Yee wei
Róisín Alexander
Rong Han
Roquas
Rosie M.
Ross Johnson - fan of the series
Ross Tipton
Rossco
rossokun
RosyMiz
Rowan Haakmeester
Rowan Reding
Rowen Andramion
Roy Knight
Ruben Blanco
RubyHarper.CN
Rueben
Rummy Sidow Moyow
Russell
Rutana

Ruthie & NeNe
Ruud
Ry Feder
Ryan Beckett
Ryan Cobb
Ryan Fajdetich
Ryan G. and Stephanie S.
Ryan Holland and Christa
Sheffield
Ryan Loree
Ryan Medlin
Ryan Myers
Ryan U.
Ryan VanLiere
Ryan Westervelt
Ryss and Silas
Ryu24-7
S. Armatage
S. Moon
S.Angel
S.L. King
Sabreena Monday
Sabrella
Saffron Eve
SageSuarez
SageVega
Sal Puma
Salman A. AlSudairy
Sam & Hayley Hart
Sam Catt
Sam Fiveash
Sam Koeser
Sam Lloyd
Sam 'Mestafa' Sanders
Sam Speciale
Samantha P
SamJam
Sammy Eu
Sammy Grumpers
Samuel Bender
Sandy Sabatino
Sania K.
Sara Marie
Sarah and Colin
Sarah Becka
Sarah Davis
Sarah E Cueto
Sarah Esker
Sarah Michele Hreha
Sarah Surya
Sarah Taub
Sarah, Asa & Ash
sarahantiqua
Sarai Porretta
Sariela
Saro Nortrup
Sasha Iris Cheer
Savannah
Savannah McKendree
Saxon Freiner
SchalaKitty
Schkan
Schnäbi93

Scott Dishnow
Scrubrova
Sean Michael-Patrick Thompson
Sean W
sebasdthamuz@gmail.com
Sebastian Bergmann
SecondBreakfastPip
Sellheim
Sepherimorth
Sgt. Skittles
ShadowC1aw18 - Potter
Shakepool
Shanna Elisei
Shannon O'Driscoll
Shao Wen Wu and Roy
Romasanta
Sharon P.
Shawn Bianchi
Shawna (Heiðinn) Sweetman
Shayla Fox / Hufflegruffon
Sheryl Goldberg
Shona and David Johnson
Shoofle Munroe
Sicorace
Sid "Neon Citizen Teal" Westrom
Sierra Rodrigues
Simon "Chillosoph" Fürst
Simon Michael Stutz
SingingSamine
Siobhan
Sir Sandwich Spread
Six31
Skep
Skookum Props & Hanamaru
Photography <3
Sky Pasko
SL-Link LOL
Sloane K
Slygirl1
snikb
Sockeye Salmon
soebadjat
Sofi Alarcon
Solokarrot
SonicKing2004
Spagonia
Sparksplitter
Spencer Dewar
Spice
Spice Nerd
Stacey Picot
Steev Hovey & Casey Withers
steezysandile
Stefanie Schulz
Stefano Triglia
Stefke
Stephanie K Watson
Stephen Bunt
Stephen Jones
Stephen Patrick
Stephen Press
Stephen Sweeney
Steve McShane

Steven & Sally
Steven B.
Steven C
Stevie Coelho
Stewart M.
Storm
Strawbeetle
student
SuddenlyToaster
SullyPwnz
Sunny Rose
Sunnygirl
SuperMCGamer
Supporter of gaming as well as
cooking
Delaney West
Chris and Bernice
Lindsey Butler
Susan E Lund
Susana Juarez & Nicholas
Wakeley
SuSu
Swashbuckling Swordmaster
Sappenfield
Sydney Hanrahan
Sydney Shea
Syra L.
Tahnee M
Talia DeMartinis
Tanalilt
Tanner (TANNAR) Gilbert
Tanner Counts
tarachu ichooseyou
Tarynn Tvo
Tasha Steele
Tatjana Lauterbach
tatompkins88
Taylor Hellmann
Taylor Ohlmann
Terry Y
Neressa and the Salazar Family
Thank You Katalin :)
The Bengrys
The Blandford Clan
The Butz
The Couchenours
The Legendary Tae Ann Towers
The Mysterious Backer 'X'
The Pirate Sheep
The thirsty gnome
TheCr4zyM4n
TheSilverHydra
Thierry Légaré
Thomas Krolikowski
Thomas Stocker
Ticcy
Tif Kieft
Tim and Kelly Troy
Tim Bocek
Tim Davick
Tim Smith
Tim Voves
Timothy Burgess

Timothy LeGower
Tina Y.
Garrett "Malibu" Zaffke
To the best sister in all of Hyrule,
Heather D.!
To the new Mark&Jackie Brandao
on this new adventure together.
"It's dangerous to go alone."
Tobi
Tobias
Tom A.
Tom Britland
Tom Plutt
Tomas Bowers
Tomat
Tommy Worthington
Tony & Ali Vessels
Tony Scimeca
Tonzog
TR Shulkcum
Tracie Henderson
Tracy D.
Travis H.
Travis Salter
Travis Short
Treble Notes
Trent Paul Brown
Trent Petronaitis
Trevor Dunlap
Trevor M
Triplicate Entertainment
Tristan R
Troll hero, J.N.
trueLove429
Turchiple
TurkeyTurk217
Turturs the Adventurer
Txi-Txi
Tye Watson
Tyler & Teresa Stuart
Tyler Anderson
Tyler H.
Tyler Marin
Tyler Ross Edwards
Tyler Shaw
Tympest Books
Tyson Hood
Ultraconmen
Unbrokenserenity
Uncle Kyky
Unexpected Noemi
UnstoppableAsh
usako
V
V Shadow
Valarie Rock
Valutie
Vanessa Stembridge
Vee!
Veronica Huber
Vianki Studios
Vicente Corbí Núñez
Vicky Wilcox

Victor Huang
Victor Page
Victoria Lauren
Vidette McClelland
Vincent GERMAIN aka Vinzius
Vincent Girard-David
Vincent Kong
Vincent Lovallo
Vincent Zhang
Violet Adelheim
VonHales
vrannicat
Wesley Ellermeijer
Western Webster
Will Myatt
William Roark
William Wood
William, House of Mechnig
Willowia Wolfmoon
Wiva
WoadWitch
Wolfesword
Wratih9
Yanni Peri-Okonny
Yau Ki Tat
Yelvious
Yiheng Shu (tcsyh)
Yijiejie
Yizhou Li, from Shanghai, China
YJ Lee
Yorick26
Vincent, Sonia, & Matteo
Romagnuolo
Nicole Pataky &Pete Romagnuolo
Josette & Santiago Abreu
Michele Renee Pace
Dottie & Frank Pace
Vicky Ferrigno
Dottie "G" Giordano
Michele & Pat Romagnuolo
弦月
让自己和家人享受美味吧
Yung Moose Rider
YuRaine
Zach Schwartz
Zachary Hicks
Zachary Hinds
Zachary Wakefield
zachery.milton
Zack Bartosh
Zak Lynch
Zanzaaa
Zeehan Shaikh
zelcheres
Zelda1fan
ZeldaandFairies
ZeldaMaster
Zeldasia
ZeldathonFR Team
Zöé "Lucky" Puchette
Zill
Zoé Pollyn
Mom and Dad

Rosemary

217

Index

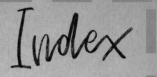

Index

-Li Kovács @LiKovacs

The Next Quest

We want to personally thank everyone for seeing through this culinary adventure. You've helped us create a product that will bring joy, new memories, and full stomachs to countless people across the globe.

-The Legend's Cookbook Team

This cookbook helped me meet amazing people who I can now call my friends. Yeah, you, Alyssa, Pat, and El Jefe. I will always cherish the memories of our cooking trips and adventures down grocery aisles, and that one time we went to a swamp and fought those seagulls on the beach. I also want to thank everyone else on the team that I got to work with. You are all so talented. Now to the reader, I just want to say thank you and look forward to our next quest. Oh, and once again thank you mom and dad!

-Peter J. Abreu

THE LEGEND'S COOKBOOK

Pinch -or- Dash

(Less than **1/8** teaspoon)

1 tablespoon = **3** teaspoons

(**15** milliliters)

For herbs...

1 Tablespoon **Fresh** = **1** teaspoon **Dry**

×16 tablespoons = **1** Cup

(**8** fluid ounces -*or*- **240** milliliters)

4 tablespoons + + + = **1/4** Cup

(**60** milliliters)

2 Tablespoons = **1** Fluid Ounce

(**30** milliliters)

8 tablespoons = **1/2** Cup
(**120** milliliters)

12 tablespoons = **3/4** Cup
(**180** milliliters)

2 cups = **1** pint
(**16** fluid ounces or **480** milliliters)

2 pints = **1** quart
(**32** fluid ounces or **1** liter)

4 quarts = **1** gallon
(**4** liters)

1 ounce = **28** grams

8 ounces = **1/2** pound
(**230** grams)

1 pound = **16** ounces
(**450** grams)

Temperature Conversions

212 °F	100 °C
275 °F	140 °C
300 °F	150 °C
325 °F	165 °C
350 °F	177 °C
375 °F	190 °C
400 °F	200 °C
425 °F	220 °C
450 °F	230 °C
475 °F	245 °C
500 °F	260 °C

Abbreviations

C, c	CUP
g	GRAM
kg	KILOGRAM
L, l	LITER
lb	POUND
mL, ml	MILLILITER
oz	OUNCE
pt	PINT
t, tsp	TEASPOON
T, TB, Tbl, Tbsp	TABLESPOON